THE LIGHTNING HORSE

John Moore

YARD DOG PRESS

The Lightning Horse
John Moore
First Edition Copyright © John Moore, 2014

This is a work of fiction. Names, characters, places, and incidents are the products of the author's imagination or are used fictitiously and are not to be construed as real. Any resemblance to actual events, locales, organizations, or persons, living or dead, is entirely coincidental.

ISBN 978-1-937105-67-9
The Lightning Horse
First Edition Copyright © John Moore, 2014

All rights reserved. No part of this book may be reproduced in any form or by any electronic or mechanical means, including information storage and retrieval systems, without permission in writing from the publisher, except by a reviewer, who may quote brief passages in a review. Any members of educational institutions wishing to photocopy part or all of the work for classroom use, or publishers who would like to obtain permission to include the work in an anthology should send their inquiries to Yard Dog Press at the address below.

Yard Dog Press
710 W. Redbud Lane
Alma, AR 72921-7247

http://www.yarddogpress.com

Edited by Selina Rosen
Copy and Technical Editor Lynn Stranathan
Cover art by Brad Foster

First Edition September 15, 2014
Printed in the United States of America
0 9 8 7 6 5 4 3 2 1

DEDICATION

To Cheryl

CHAPTER ONE

Yellow arcs flashed over the mountains. Thunder bounced between the peaks and echoed off canyon walls, turning each BOOM into a cannonade of boom boom booms. Down in the village of Barrenstock a cold rain was already falling, but the brunt of the storm was still to come. Rivulets of chill water ran between the paving stones. Gusts of wind blew between the stone houses, whipping droplets off the eaves and splattering them against the windows. Bedraggled cats slunk from doorway to doorway. Balustrade Barley, full time innkeeper and part time mayor of Barrenstock, stood in the entrance of his inn and pulled his oilskin around his belly. Only complete and utter fools, he decided, would venture out in a storm like this. With a sigh he resigned himself to the fact that he was going to have to join them.

He considered returning to his kitchen and fortifying himself with a tankard of hot broth before going out into the wet. He cast a glance over his shoulder, to his warm and well-lit dining room. His wife looked sternly back at him. He grimaced, shoved his hands deep in his pockets and hurried across the square. A large group of villagers, comprising pretty much most of the town, were already gathered. They were armed with pitchforks. Some carried torches. They seemed oblivious to the rain, too wound up to feel the cold. He pushed his way to the center of the crowd. "For goodness sake, Martin," he said. "What's with the torches? It's barely afternoon."

"You always bring torches when you're storming a castle," said Martin. He was tall and lean and was not wearing a hat today, so his wet hair was plastered to his head, giving his bony face a skull-like appearance. "That's just the way it's done. Anyway, it might be dark before we're finished."

"We have lanterns, you know. And why are you bringing pitchforks? What are you going to do, clean out his stable?"

"Pitchforks, too. You've got to have pitchforks for this sort of thing. You always bring pitchforks."

Around him, the other villagers nodded. Storming a castle just wasn't the same without torches and pitchforks.

"Put the pitchforks away," said Barley. "We don't want any accidents. It's a steep road, and it will be slippery. Someone could fall and hurt himself. We don't want a repeat of last time."

"We need weapons," said Martin grimly.

"You don't need weapons. Who are you going to fight? It's just the two of them up there tonight. The Doctor and Andy. And Andy is just a kid."

"Really?" said Martin. He dropped his voice and fixed his eyes on the mayor. The villagers gathered closer. "And what about the monster?"

Involuntarily, Barley looked up at the castle. He couldn't see it clearly, as it was shrouded in fog and drizzle, but the gray outline was there, and a few lights glimmered in the windows. "There isn't—you don't know that—we can't be sure—oh, come on, everyone. It's cold and it's wet and none of us really want to go trekking up the mountain, do we? There's no immediate danger. Come inside the inn and have some hot cider. Tomorrow I'll go to the castle and talk with the Doctor. I'm sure we can calmly get to the bottom of this."

"Tomorrow will be too late," charged Martin. He waved a hand in the direction of Castle Lachtenslachter. "Look at it." They all looked, and at that moment a long and jagged fork of lightning backlit the castle, so that it stood out, grim and foreboding, against the dark clouds. Martin, Barley remembered, had an irritating aptitude for excellent timing.

"He needs the lightning!" shouted Martin, "to power his infernal devices! Look you now, the storm is moving up the valley. In yet an hour it will be upon us." His voice rose another ten decibels. "We dare not tarry. Can you not sense it? Can you not sense the evil that emanates from that place of madness?" He raised one arm straight over his head, and then dramatically snapped it down so his hand was pointing at the castle. "Look at it, crouched over our village like a giant fiend, and feel the horror that rises from its black stones."

His performance was hokey but effective. The villagers responded by waving their pitchforks and shouting their agreement. Instead of dampening their spirits, the cold rain seemed to add to their anger. Barley had to raise his voice to make himself heard. "It's the same castle now as on any sunny day," he called out. "There's nothing mysterious about it, and certainly nothing horrifying. It's just a castle. You've all been inside at one time or another. Mrs. Barley was up there just this morning, delivering a cake."

"Yes!" shouted someone. "What kind of cake?"

Barley hesitated. The crowd fell quiet, waiting for his answer. More people had arrived in the last few minutes. They pushed their way forward, forcing the crowd into a dense circle around the mayor. They were all there now, the whole village, every man and woman who could get a babysitter that night, all watching him. A few drops of water found their way under his collar and trickled down his back. "A birthday cake," he admitted.

"There, you see!" shouted Martin. "Do we not know what that means?" Another flash of lightning lit his face. "Has experience taught us nothing? The time is now. We must act quickly, before these torches burn down." A peal of thunder underscored his words. "To the castle!"

"To the castle," roared the villagers.

The mob made its decision. A few who were closest to the castle road started in that direction. The rest followed. Those who had pitchforks waved them angrily. Those villagers who didn't own pitchforks had rented them just for this occasion, leaving behind a hefty deposit. Others had to improvise with shovels, brooms and mops. A couple of upstairs maids brandished their feather dusters. Martin lifted his torch and hurried to the front of the procession. "Follow me," he shouted.

"Yes, great. Excellent leadership, Martin," muttered Barley. He went back to his inn, where his wife Evelyn was still watching from the doorway. She stood aside to let him through. He gave her a resigned look as he edged past, and she gave him a sympathetic look, and he turned and looked disconsolately at the crowd of villagers moving in a loose pack up the mountain road, torchlight gleaming off wet, angry faces, a trail of sparks streaming behind them. He was about to turn away when another group of men, a dozen or more in two columns, younger, stronger, tougher than the rest of the pack, emerged from a side street. They had rope slings across their shoulders, and suspended between the columns was a heavy, muddy log. Barley watched them follow the pack up toward the castle, until the two groups merged together. It was only then that he realized what he had just seen.

"Oh no," he said out loud. "Not the ... not the battering ram!" And he hurried after them.

"Clamp," Doctor Lachtenslachter said.

Andy swept a lock of ash–blonde hair out of his eyes with the sleeve of his operating gown. He selected a clamp from a wooden tray of steel surgical tools, and passed it to the surgeon. "Clamp," he repeated.

"Scalpel."

"Scalpel."

"Retractor."

"Retractor."

Lachtenslachter drew his blade away from an incision. Special candle lamps, with metal reflectors and polished lenses, threw halos of light on the operating table. The subject of their efforts was draped with sheets, so only a small patch of skin, the area where Lachtenslachter was operating, was visible. The hair had been shaved to expose only clean skin. The Doctor used no gas, no chloroform, no anesthesia at all. Yet in spite of this, the patient did not flinch from the knife. In fact, there was no movement at all, not even a sign of breath. "Give me his vital stats, Andy."

His teenage assistant looked at the manometer. "Blood pressure zero. Respiration zero. Pulse zero."

"Good, good." Having confirmed that the patient's condition was stable, Lachtenslachter felt free to continue with the operation.

"Glue," he said. Andy handed him a tube.

"String."

"String."

"Paper clip. Sealing wax." He worked swiftly, completing the procedure in a little less than ten minutes. Then he stood back with a smile of satisfaction. "I think that should take care of it. I have a good feeling about this one, Andy. Do you want to close him up?"

"Sure," said Andy, pleased to be given the responsibility. He switched places with the middle-aged surgeon, but Lachtenslachter stayed at his shoulder and watched him carefully.

"Remember what I taught you, Andy. What's the most important thing every doctor needs to remember?"

"Grip your golf club with your fingers, not with your palms."

"Um, right, but aside from that. When completing a procedure?"

"Don't leave any surgical supplies inside the patient." Andy probed inside the wound with a forceps, removed the ball of string and put it on the tray. "I saw this, Doctor Lachtenslachter. I know you were testing me."

"We all need to be tested, Andy. It keeps us on our toes."

Andy continued with the forceps. "And these two coins. And this ring. And this corkscrew. I assume these were all part of the test?"

"The corkscrew is in there? I wondered where that got to." Lachtenslachter saw Andy's expression. "Just kidding, Andy. Yes, it was part of test. You can go ahead and close up now. How is my niece doing?

"Deedee has been waiting in the hall for hours. She's very worried. You know how much she wants to see him."

"And I told her she can't see him until it's over." Lachtenslachter stripped off his surgical gloves. "The storm is coming up fast and we still have preparations to make. Well, finish up here while I go out and tell her the operation was a success ..."

"Although the patient," finished Andy, "is still dead."

In the valley the rain was mild and warm. A man in a checked suit, pork pie hat, and spectator shoes leaned on the rail at Geht Downs racetrack, watching the horses parade past him on their way to the starting gate, ready to run the last race of the day. He went by the name of Phil "Finishline" Finster. He liked being up at the rail. A lot of gamblers didn't care much to actually watch a horserace. They only cared about the results. Finishline was different. He liked horses and he liked the spectacle of racing, and he especially liked to stand at the finish line when the horses came in a pack, thousands of pounds of bone and muscle and sinew thundering toward him at forty miles per hour, flanks throwing off sweat and hooves tossing up clods of dirt, and the skinny young jockeys hunched over their necks and urging them forward. Finishline was certain that nothing else in the world was quite as exciting.

He was feeling pretty good. The track was muddy, but that was okay with Finishline. He had some money on a bay horse called the Roan Ranger, and the Roan Ranger was a good mudder. In fact, the Roan Ranger was good on all types of turf. So it was short odds, and the payout wouldn't be great, but Finishline had already won some money that day and he was content to win just a little more. None of the other horses were in the same class as the Roan Ranger.

He tilted his hat forward so the rain would run off the front and not down his back. The water, dripping off the brim right in front of his eyes, sobered his mood a little. He reflected that the money he won today was a drop in the bucket compared to the amount of money he still owed. Especially since he owed most of that money to Werner Waxroth.

It was unfortunate. Finishline knew how he could get the money. He had received a tip on a horse that was, in the words of the tipster, as close to a sure thing as anything was likely to be sure. This guy who gave him the tip had a friend who was brother to a guy who worked in the stables with this particular horse, so there was no doubt that this was the inside dope. But there was a problem. The problem was that a guy has to bet big money to win big money and Finishline did not have big money to bet, his cash flow being more than somewhat negative at this time. A lot of guys in Finishline's position would have been darting their eyes around the stands and looking nervously over their shoulders. Finishline didn't have to watch his back. He had his doll, Goldie, to watch it for him. So he turned his attention back to the track and watched the horses getting into post position.

Despite his problems, thinking of Goldie made him smile. She had won a little money herself that day, so they were in good shape for the time being, with enough cash for a nice dinner and maybe to pay something on their room at the inn, although normally Finishline did not like to waste hard won money on frivolities such as rent. He smiled even more when he felt her hand on his neck. He stopped smiling when he heard her nervous voice. "Um, Finishline?" He turned around.

Goldie was standing very straight and looking very unhappy. She was standing very straight because a huge man had grabbed a bunch of her hair, twisted it around one giant fist, and was holding it so Goldie had to stand on her toes. This, undoubtedly, was why she looked so upset. The strain on her hair also pulled up the skin of her forehead, and her eyebrows, making her look wide-eyed and innocent, which was very definitely something that Goldie was not.

"Well hello, Grogan," said Finishline, giving the big man a big smile. "I see you are putting the arm on my ever-loving fiancée, Mrs. Goldie Theis, who is finding the situation very upsetting. I am also more than somewhat disturbed, and seeing as it is my marker that Werner Waxroth is carrying, I think it is very unfair of you and certainly an ungentlemanly and no-good thing to do, to treat Goldie this way, and furthermore you are ruining a particularly nice hairdo, which is very difficult for a woman to maintain on a rainy day such as this. I would count it very much a personal favor if you would release Goldie's hair and put the arm on me, if you think someone needs the arm put on him."

"I'm not putting the arm on either of you," said Grogan. "Not yet, anyway. This was just an attention–getter." He released Goldie's hair suddenly, causing her to rock back on her heels, and her breasts to bob up and down several times before she regained her balance. "I wanted to get her attention, because I wanted to get your attention, before she got your attention first and let you know I was looking for you." All this came out in a voice that rumbled like a kettle drum with indigestion. "It seems that some people have complained that you're getting hard to find, Finishline. They started to think you might be avoiding them. People's feeling get hurt if they think their old friends are avoiding them. Especially people like Mr. Waxroth. He's very sensitive about these things."

When he was a child, someone had told Grogan's mother that her son had the size and shape of a sack of potatoes. At the time that was completely true. Now that he was a grown man, Grogan had a build like a very large sack of coconuts, in the sense that he bulged in a lot of places and the bulges were extremely hard. Finishline, on the other hand, looked like a man you would not back in a shadow–boxing competition. Goldie slipped behind him anyway. Finishline stood in front of her in a protective manner, although considering the threat he was facing, he actually offered about the same amount of protection that a white picket fence provides against a charging bison.

"Well, Grogan, I certainly do not want Werner Waxroth to have the mistaken impression that I do not want the pleasure of his company. Especially since this mistaken impression is not true. Werner Waxroth is a man for whom I have the greatest amount of respect. It is just that I am more than somewhat busy with business these days and this accounts for the lack of attention I am giving to my colleagues. In fact, I am just now planning to see Werner Waxroth and pay a little something on my marker."

"Mr. Waxroth would like it better if you paid more than a little something on your marker. He'd like it better if you paid the whole thing."

"I think that is something we can both agree on, although I must explain that business is very bad these days. But you know that I am a not a person who welshes on a bet, although there are a few times when I am regrettably delayed in settling up, and Werner Waxroth knows that very well." This was true. Sooner or later—generally later—Finishline had always managed to scrape together enough cash to redeem his markers. Except that Finishline and Goldie and Waxroth and Grogan all knew that Finishline had never been this deep in debt before, or this late in making payment. It was entirely possible that Waxroth might consider him more useful as an example to other clients than as a source of revenue.

"Then as long as you are going to see Mr. Waxroth there is no need for me to stick around," said Grogan. "I'll let Mr. Waxroth know you're coming. I'll tell him you'll be waiting outside his office right after the last race. This race. Right after. So that just in case you lose your way and don't show up, he can send me to find you." This was meant to have an undertone of menace. It certainly did so, although it also had overtones of menace and a few tones of peril, hazard, and jeopardy through the mid-range. Grogan could not have been less subtle if he had threatened the two of them with a fireman's ax.

"I am coming to see him right after I collect my winnings," said Finishline. "A thing of which I am very much looking forward to do. Although in this case the race is such a foregone conclusion that the track might as well open the payout window now."

"I don't bet myself," said Grogan. "Mr. Waxroth doesn't allow it. For example, if I was betting money on Common Valor to win this race, which I've heard is a good bet, people might think I was placing a bet for Mr. Waxroth. And we all know that Mr. Waxroth has no connection with racing."

Finishline turned around to see Goldie giving him a significant look. He switched his gaze to the horses, which were now at the starting gate. The Roan Ranger had the rail position. He was a beautiful bay, healthy and eager. Muscles rippled beneath his glossy coat. Finishline turned back to Grogan. "That is no doubt a good policy, particularly as Common Valor could not win this race if all the other horses were hobbled and running around the track backward."

"Horse racing is full of surprises," said Grogan. He pushed his way through the crowd, or more accurately, the crowd quickly got out of his path as he walked away. Goldie pursed her lips.

"You know, Finishline," she said thoughtfully. "It occurs to me—just a suspicion really—but some inner sixth sense tells me that Waxroth is upset with us."

"I have much the same thought, sweetheart. Of more immediate concern, however, is this: Do you have an investment on Common Valor?"

"No, of course not." She was interrupted by the clang of the starting bell. Across the track the horses charged out of the gates in a shower of mud. "Common Valor is seven years old. He hasn't finished in the money in two years. He's not a mudder. He's eighteen to one against. He's on his way to the glue factory."

The voice of the caller interrupted her. Finishline watched intently. Toucan Play was first out of the gate and galloped to a good start, but was quickly passed by Meretricious. The Roan Ranger led the rest of the pack, but in the backstretch left them behind and quickly closed the distance between himself and the two leaders. Common Valor trailed the pack. Finishline chewed his lip. It was just what he expected. So why did Grogan mention Common Valor?

He found out when the horses reached the home stretch. The Roan Ranger passed Toucan Play in the far turn and was closing on Meretricious, when the lead horse stumbled and went down. The Roan Ranger was going too fast, and was too close to stop. He ran into Meretricious and went down also. Toucan Play's jockey tried to turn it. It slipped in the mud and went down. The other jockeys pulled on their reins and desperately tried to avoid the pileup. It all happened in a moment, and all Finishline could see were flailing hooves and wet bodies sliding through the mud. And Common Valor, hugging the outside rail, continued on to be first past the post.

It wasn't the first time that either Finishline or Goldie had seen a horse stumble on the track, especially a wet track. They had also seen pileups before. But even they were stunned at the suddenness and size of the disaster. Goldie stood on tiptoe, trying to see over the crowd of people that had rushed to the rail. "Finishline, can you see? Are any of the jockeys hurt?"

Finishline waited to answer until he was certain. Racing was a dangerous business. Two jockeys were limping. One was lying down but was able to lift his head. National Cordy, the famous girl jockey, had dismounted and was kneeling by his side. A stretcher team ran onto the track. "I think they are all okay this time. They are getting up." One of the fallen horses rose. One of them stayed down. The Roan Ranger struggled to its feet and tried to walk. It limped badly. A track official grabbed its reins.

"That," said Finishline, "does not bode well for the future of that horse." He took a betting slip from his pocket and tore it up.

"How did he do it?"

"Who?"

"Waxroth," said Goldie. "It was Waxroth. I know it. You know it, too. I don't know how he fixed it, but he did."

Finishline looked at the Roan Ranger, but his eyes were unfocused. He seemed lost in thought. Without turning around, he reached his hand toward her.

Goldie took his arm. "Come on, Finishline. We had better go and see Waxroth before he sends someone after us again."

Finishline shook his head. "Right this minute an idea occurs to me, Goldie. How much money do we have?"

The center of the storm was coming up fast. Andy watched it from a window. Heavy clouds put the afternoon landscape into gloomy shadow, but periodically great sheets of lightning illuminated the cliffs and lit up the dense stands of fir and spruce. Outside, he knew, thunder was cracking and booming, wild animals were sheltering in their burrows, farm animals were shifting nervously in their stalls, dogs were cowering under tables, and cats were hiding under sofas with their fur standing on end. But inside the Castle Lachtenslachter he could hear only dull rumbles. The thick stone walls and heavy glass windows provided shelter from noise as well as the elements.

He did not think to look out the opposite windows, in the direction of the village.

"The storm is coming right at us, Doctor Lachtenslachter," he said. "Are you ready? How are the new electrodes holding up?"

"Just fine, Andy." Doctor Lachtenslachter wiped his hands on his laboratory coat, leaving a smear of blood and embalming fluid. "I have a good feeling about using silver instead of copper. They conduct electricity better, and they'll look so much classier after it comes to life, especially if they're kept polished." Andy knew the creature had been ready for days, waiting for the right storm to bring it to life, but Lachtenslachter kept tinkering with it right up to the last moment. "I want this one to be perfect," he told Andy.

Andy looked out the window some more. Gusts of wind

shook the trees in the forest. "This is a violent storm, Doctor Lachtenslachter I don't think we've ever opened up to one this heavy before." He turned his back on the window and looked around the laboratory. It had once been the castle library, a room that stretched up two stories, with sliding ladders that led to a mezzanine. It still had a few leather club chairs, although these had been pushed off to one side. There was a high scrivener's desk, where Lachtenslachter made his notes, so he could write without having to sit down. The ceiling had an array of skylights to brighten the room for reading. The shelves were made of oak, much of it elaborately carved. Andy had no doubt that Lachtenslachter's ancestors had paid dearly for those shelves, but now the wood was so stained with chemicals that any value had long ago disappeared. They still held a lot of books—the latest works of chemistry, anatomy, physiology—as well as Lachtenslachter's own bound notes, a couple of mystery novels, and his golf trophies. And they also held racks of surgical instruments, tubs of preserving fluid, glass jars of grotesque body parts, bottles of plasma and saline, and a pair of pet goldfish in a bowl. The creature, still draped in white linen sheets, was lying on the oversized operating table. Copper cables, wrapped in cloth insulation, ran from under the sheets to an array of iron lightning rods located across the floor. Behind the operating table a half dozen brass gauges were mounted into a maple rack. At this time all their needles still registered zero.

"We'll have to take a chance with the storm, Andy." Doctor Lachtenslachter caught a pair of thick rubber gloves from his assistant. "I've installed fusible links in the cables. They should give us additional protection when the lightning strikes."

Andy donned his own gloves. "Are you going to scream, 'Life, give my creation life' again?"

"Of course. This is a special occasion. We'll wait for lightning to strike, I'll do the scream, the creature will rise from the table, and we'll sing Happy Birthday and have some cake. Give me a hand with these rods, would you please, Andy?"

Andy helped him set the rods into a rack, fitting the ends into ceramic insulators. He tied ropes to the eyebolts in the ends of the rack. "Remember to lift with your legs, Andy, not with your back."

"I know." The rods weren't heavy so much as unwieldy. When they were in position, Lachtenslachter gave Andy a nod, and Andy went up a ladder to the mezzanine, then up another ladder to open one of the skylights. He looked down to see if the Doctor was ready. Lachtenslachter pulled back a sheet to reveal the creature's head. He picked up one end of a copper cable. Carefully he connected it to one of the creature's electrodes with a spring clamp. He took a second cable and did the same to the other electrode. He put a stethoscope to the creature's inert chest and thumped it. Satisfied, he looked up and gave Andy the OK sign. They both put on safety goggles. Andy opened the skylight.

Neither of them was quite prepared for the violence of the storm. The noise level jumped abruptly, as the room filled with the sound of rolling thunder and the drumming of rain on a slate roof. It soaked Andy's head and shoulders in a moment. Lachtenslachter hustled to get his notebooks out of harm's way. Hard cold drops came in through the opening, rattling on the operating table and soaking the sheets, so that they clung to the creature's muscular legs. Had they been listening carefully they might have noticed, almost lost in the din, the faint tramp of villagers' boots, and the mayor's distant voice, "Not the battering ram, damn it! Those are antique doors!" But they were engrossed in their project.

Andy wiped the water out of his eyes. A brace of pulleys hung beneath the skylight. He grabbed the rope nearest him and waited for Lachtenslachter to begin. When the Doctor began pulling on the second rope, Andy matched his pace, so that the rack of long iron rods rose to the ceiling. It took several minutes of hauling to get the rack up to the ceiling. Andy tugged on it to position it beneath the open skylight. A minute later the lightning rods protruded through the roof. He tied off his rope and slid down the ladders.

Lachtenslachter wrote the time down in his notebook. "Stay away from the ropes," he cautioned Andy. "They're wet, and they might—good Lord!"

Andy knew what he meant. The laboratory suddenly filled with blue light. It engulfed the rods and ran down the ropes, burning them, it appeared, without consuming them. Above the rain and thunder Andy heard a crackling noise. He looked up to see the blue fire jump to the chandelier, putting a glowing halo above their heads. Blue light danced over every metal surface, an effect more magical than any stage show he had ever seen. Then the blue light vanished, as suddenly and mysteriously as it had appeared.

"Saint Elmo's fire," said Lachtenslachter with wonderment.

He made a note of it. "I've heard sailors speak of it. Careful."

Andy felt his scalp tingle. He looked at his arms and saw the hairs rising. He saw Lachtenslachter's hair standing on end also, but the Doctor's hair did that a lot anyway. Still, this was the most dangerous part of the procedure. The air was heavy with static electrical charge.

"Stay alert. Any time now ..." began Lachtenslachter. The lightning cut him off, a tremendous bolt, far stronger than anything they had encountered in their previous experiments, and it seemed to last forever. The creature on the table gave a single, convulsive jerk before the rack holding the lightning rods exploded in flame, the rods themselves spattering molten metal as they crashed, white hot, to the floor. Instinctively, both Andy and the Doctor threw their arms over their heads. The instruments spun off their dials and shattered. Three windows blew out in a shower of glass spicules. Wind and rain rushed in. Candles went out. The oil lamp toppled, splashing burning whale oil across the floor. Andy yanked off his laboratory coat and beat out the flames. Lachtenslachter did the same, pulling off his own coat and helping Andy. Quick work put the fire out, but it left them in darkness.

In darkness, yet only for a moment.

The laboratory door was thrown open with such force that it slammed against the wall. Villagers poured in, filling the room with angry shouts and the flickering light of their torches. They waved their pitchforks and dust mops threateningly. "Doctor Lachtenslachter, stop!" yelled Martin. "You must stop this madness."

They were too late. On the operating table, the creature stirred. The shrouds slipped from its head, uncovering one large, staring eye. Its legs thumped spasmodically against the marble table. It began to rise. The villagers backed away, plastering themselves against the bookshelves.

"Life!" screamed Lachtenslachter. "Give my creation life!"

His words were underscored by a final crack of lightning. The creature turned over and rose to its knees. The copper cables sparked and fell away from the electrodes in its head. It shuddered several times, its head shaking spastically, but then it seemed to get control of itself, and smoothly rose to its feet. The sheets dropped away, to reveal a powerful body and deep chest, covered with short, white hair. Thick lips curled away from ungainly yellow teeth. It stood on the operating table, looked calmly around the room and let out a long snort.

"My God," said Martin. "It's ..." He had to pause for a moment to let his mind grapple with the unexpected sight. "It's a pony?"

"Yes," said Lachtenslachter calmly. "I promised my niece a pony for her birthday. Deedee, where are you?"

A little girl slipped through the crowd. She wore a clean, starched pinafore. Her hair was tied back with pink ribbon. She stood before the pony and looked at it with awe. "He's beautiful."

"Andy, close the skylight, please."

Andy was already on a ladder, unfurling a roll of oiled paper and tacking it over the broken windows. "I'm on my way, Doctor Lachtenslachter. Deedee, be careful of the broken glass."

Deedee climbed up on the table. She hugged the pony, which nuzzled her shoulder. "Look, he likes me. I'm going to name him Patches, because he's all different colors."

Barley shoved his way through the mass of villagers. "Nice going, Martin," he said, clapping the man on the shoulder. "Now, tell the Doctor exactly what we're all doing here. Tell him what you planned to do to this little girl's pony. On her birthday."

Martin swallowed. "Well, I thought—we all thought—um, Doctor Lachtenslachter?" Martin swept his hand around the room to take in all the equipment—the Leyden jars, the electrophorus condensers, the Ramsden plate generator. "Surely you could have just *bought* a pony for less than it cost to set up all this?"

"Of course," said Lachtenslachter. "But you appreciate it more when you make it yourself."

"I helped," said Deedee proudly.

"And you did a wonderful job," Barley told her. "It's a lovely pony."

Deedee looked at the villagers curiously, seeming to notice them for the first time. Once again they backed toward the door, although slowly this time, now out of embarrassment rather than fear. "Did you come for my birthday party?"

There was a breath of silence. Until Barley said, "Yes, Deedee. Yes, we did. Happy birthday, Deedee." This was followed by a chorus of happy birthdays.

Andy came down from the mezzanine. "And tell her why you brought the torches." He grinned at various villagers who were attempting to hide torches and pitchforks behind their backs.

"We ran out of birthday candles," one of them said. The other villagers nodded. Someone began singing the birthday song. The rest of the group, including Barley, Martin, the Doctor, and Andy, all joined in. Deedee stroked the pony's mane and looked very happy.

"Deedee," said Andy, when they were finished. "Why don't I take you and Patches to the stable now?" He lifted her onto the pony's back. Barley helped him move a ramp to the table so the pony could walk down. "Then we'll come back and everyone will have some cake."

Deedee nodded, her ponytail bobbing behind her. "Uncle Albert, may I sleep in the stable tonight, so Patches won't be lonely?"

"Yes, but only for tonight. And come back in and wash up first."

The villagers took this as a signal to leave. They mumbled apologies for their unplanned presence to Lachtenslachter. A few added half-hearted excuses about just being in the neighborhood with a pitchfork and wondering if the Doctor had any hay he wanted put up. Martin led the way out the door, this time not waiting to see where the crowd went first. Barley was the last to leave. He shook his head regretfully as he stood at a window and watched his fellow villagers depart. But when he turned to survey the laboratory and the mass of damaged equipment, his face grew sterner. He spoke to Andy in a low voice. "Mark my words, Andy. One of these days the two of you will go too far with your experiments. There are some things mankind was not meant to know."

"Really?" Andy was interested. "What are they?"

"Um, I don't know."

"Right. Right, of course. Wait, you didn't batter down the front door again, did you?"

"No," said Barley quickly. "We used the spare key hidden in the garden."

"Because we had so much trouble with the insurance company last time."

"Yes, I remember. The door is fine."

"Yes, well, good evening Mr. Mayor. Nice of you to drop by."

There was an exchange of pleasantries, then Barley left. The center of the storm had passed over by now, leaving only mild rain. Andy and the Doctor set to work cleaning up. It was close to midnight by the time they had the equipment stowed away, the operating table scrubbed, the glass swept up, and oiled paper tacked up over the rest of the broken windows. Deedee had long since gone to bed. They retired to the kitchen, where Andy made coffee, and they both sat down to finish off the last of the birthday cake.

"You know, Andy." Lachtenslachter, wiped a trace of frosting from his lips. "Barrenstock is a nice enough village and all, but sometimes I can't help wondering if the inhabitants aren't a bit mad."

Andy had to agree.

CHAPTER TWO

The tiny country of Travaillia was, on the whole, an agreeable place to live, allowing most of its citizens a wholesome–family–value, happily–ever–after, fluffy–bunny sort of lifestyle. Every country, however, can also provide sinister stories and for Travaillia, those tales centered in the mountains. The mountains of Travaillia had an eerie reputation. The valleys were pleasant enough. Sheep grazed, orchards grew, and the sun shone on lush, green meadows that were well-watered by clear mountain streams. But those streams ran down from dark, wooded slopes, and sprang forth from darker caves, where all manner of strange beasts were rumored to lurk. Those forests, it was rumored, were the haunts of the where wolves—men who gained lupine tendencies at the time of the new moon. So it was always too dark to actually *see* them, but everyone was sure they were out there, somewhere.

And the highest cliffs, it was said, once held the castle of the evil Vlad the Enabler. This legendary count never really hurt anyone himself, but he encouraged his victims in their own self-destructive habits.

So it was not surprising that Finishline Finster and Gwendolyn "Goldie" Theis, upon driving their cart into Barrenstock's main—and only—street, hesitated before proceeding to the Castle Lachtenslachter. The cart was covered with a tarp on top, and was dripping water from the bottom. Their horse was sweating from pulling the cart up the mountain road, but a cold mountain breeze swept through the narrow street, so Finishline got down from the cart and put a blanket over the horse. Goldie was protected by a coat of red fox, which she pulled tightly around her. Finishline hunched himself into his checked jacket. He studied the castle, noted how it loomed over the town from its short summit, and speculated briefly on its property value. The clouds of the previous night had cleared away, leaving the castle backlit by bright sunlight. There was nothing particularly forbidding about the sight, nothing overtly sinister, but a castle that casts a shadow over you never really looks friendly and inviting. Finishline switched his gaze to the Barrenstock Inn.

"I do not know how you are feeling about the matter, Sweetcakes," he said, "but I am more than somewhat hungry at this time and a bite of something to eat will not be unwelcome. I do not want to face this doctor with my stomach growling. Furthermore our horse appears to be thirsty. A cool libation from the trough in front of this inn will be just the thing to wet his whistle."

"I could do with something to eat, Finishline," admitted Goldie. They had started out before dawn, for it was a long ride into the mountains, and Goldie was not in the habit of eating breakfast, partly in order to keep her figure, mostly because she rarely got up early enough for it. She waited while Finishline parked the cart, unhitched the horse, and extended a hand to help her down. "Also, it might be a good idea to ask some questions, if there is anyone around here to ask. We can find out a little more about this—scientist? Is that what you called him?"

"It is a modern term," said Finishline. "For what were once called natural philosophers. They are not sorcerers. They do not do magic. Which is indeed fortunate for us, if this guy can do magical things without doing magic, since that is the type of guy we are seeking." The inn had a door with blue paint, a brass handle, and white wooden letters that said "Inn." Underneath the white letters was a small bronze plaque that said "Mayor." Beneath it was another bronze plaque that said "Postmaster." Beneath that was a smaller bronze plaque that said "Notary." Finishline pushed the door open and held it for Goldie while she walked inside.

Barley stood behind the counter, wearing his postmaster cap, reading a letter. It had been brought down from the castle late in the morning, and was written in a child's block printing. "Dear Mr. Mayor," it said, "and everyone in Barrenstock. Thank you for the lovely battering ram. It was just what I wanted. I'm sure I'll get a lot of use out of it. Your friend, Deedee."

Barley left the front counter, crossed through the kitchen, and stuck his head out the back door. A trio of workmen was repointing the brick that formed the inn's foundation. "Jason," he called to the closest one. "What did you do with that big log that you and the boys brought up to the castle?"

"Left it there," came the answer. "The road was too slippery to bring it down last night. It was still raining. We'll get it later."

"You might have to rethink that," said Barley. "Talk to me

when you're finished." He went back inside and put the letter on the counter where Evelyn could read it. The front door opened. The Mayor of Barrenstock automatically straightened his apron, took off his postmaster cap, and put on his genial host face.

The couple that came in was a few years short of middle age. The man wore a wool suit that displayed, in Barley's opinion, a rather loud pattern, a felt hat with a turned up brim, and city shoes. It was obvious that the shoes and the hat had been expensive when new, and it was equally obvious that this had been some time ago. His companion was a woman for whom the term "brass blond" could have been coined. She walked with an unconscious wiggle and, when the man helped her out of her fur coat, displayed the kind of cleavage that makes married women shoot warning glances at their husbands. Barley introduced himself as the proprietor and showed them to a table.

"What can I get for you?" he asked, pulling out chairs. He waited until they were seated before continuing. "But first let me enquire if you will be wanting rooms tonight? Can I assist with your baggage? Are you visiting someone here in Barrenstock?"

"It's more of a business trip," said Goldie.

"My girlfriend has stated the proposition correctly," said Finishline. "For while we are enjoying the scenic splendor in the immediate environs of your fair village, we cannot help but notice that there is a castle on that hill nearby. And we have heard a rumor that the occupant of that castle is no slouch with the scalpel and bone saw, and if that is true than I am not remiss in thinking we might have a job of work for him."

They were both surprised at the reaction this got from their host, for the Mayor showed immediate suspicion, and did a quick count out loud of their visible body parts. "Arms, legs, hands, fingers, ears, all there?" He looked under the table. "Feet, one pair each?" Barley relaxed a bit when he saw no obviously missing limbs. "Please excuse my impertinence. We've had some trouble with the Doctor over this matter and finally had to pass a local regulation. Everyone who visits Doctor Lachtenslachter must leave with the same number of body parts they arrived with."

"I think that's a good law," said Goldie.

"I have no hesitation agreeing with you," said Finishline. "I myself prefer to keep all my body parts attached to my torso and furthermore, I like to avoid putting additional holes in the body I am inhabiting."

"And, if you don't mind my asking," continued Barley, "you're not by any chance carrying human cadavers in that cart of yours, are you?"

"*Human* cadavers?" said Finishline quickly. "Certainly not."

Goldie looked concerned. "Excuse me, Mr. Mayor. Are you telling us that this doctor hacks body parts off his visitors?"

"Well, not until he pays for them. He gives a good price too, I'm told. You would be surprised what people will sell when they are desperate for money."

"Actually, we probably wouldn't," said Goldie. She gave Finishline an uncomfortable look.

"And he didn't hack them off. He did a nice, neat job. But you really must hear the whole story to understand."

"I am a sucker for a good story," said Finishline. "And indeed I do not object to gaining a little more information about this Doctor Lachtenslachter."

"It is a long story ..."

"However, Goldie here tells me she has a hairdresser's appointment this very evening, and I myself want to get back to the city before the evening traffic."

"... but I don't mind telling it."

"An important appointment," said Goldie. "Back in the city. The stylist is booked up and I don't want to miss my appointment. Which is back in the city."

Barley had already drawn up a chair for himself. "Doctor Lachtenslachter was a man with an obsession."

Doctor Lachtenslachter was, or perhaps is, the most brilliant surgeon in recorded history (explained Barley). His knowledge was immense, his diagnosis unfailingly accurate. From stethoscope to scalpel, his skill was second to none. Physicians and surgeons from across the world flocked to his operating theatre to observe his techniques. Professional journals begged for his articles. Professional societies showered him with awards. He is the author of that famous book on surgery, *Remove It Now, You Don't Really Need It And It Will Prevent Complications Later In Life*, a volume that has become the standard for the medical profession, and his advances in the field of elective surgery made him the despair of insurance companies the world over.

But Lachtenslachter was a man with an obsession. It started as mere idea, but an idea that grew like a pernicious weed in an over fertile garden. The feeling was a long time in developing, but one day he reached the point where his career, successful though it was, did not satisfy him. It was no longer enough to save lives. He wanted to create life.

Yes, create life. Not merely to reanimate dead flesh, not to generate a mere zombie under the control of a necromancer's spell, but real life, able to breathe and move and sustain itself of its own will. He knew of Lord Galvan's experiments in making frog muscle twitch through the application of an electric current, and this inspired him. Electricity, he decided, was the secret of life.

He sold his practice and returned here, the ancestral castle of the Lachtenslachter family. He had spent many a summer here, working on his medical research. Now he prepared to spend the winter. Day after day, wagons of expensive equipment and rare chemicals were delivered to his door. He laid in a supply of extra firewood, food, and heavy quilts. He was cut off when the snowdrifts buried the roads, but from the village we could see lamps flickering in the windows. Night after night he pored over books and correspondence from medical authorities. The following summer he had his nephew Andy running copper cables through the walls of the Castle Lachtenslachter, and installing iron rods on the roof. We watched, of course. We had misgivings, but we kept them to ourselves. We are a tolerant lot, here in Barrenstock, and not given to interfere with a man's private business.

Until the grave–robbings began. That was too much. Then we had to put our collective foot down.

I went to see him myself. He was pale and haggard, dark circles under his eyes, hair and beard unkempt, the very portrait of a man who has been working too hard and sleeping too little. "Doctor Lachtenslachter," I told him, "this has got to stop." He argued with me, but I was firm. I told him that we are not backwards here in Barrenstock. That we understand the importance of dissection to medical science. But that robbing our local graves would not be tolerated. We agreed that from then on all cadavers had to be shipped in from out of town.

Here Barley paused his story while Evelyn set the table with a pitcher of cider, a plate of sliced brown bread, and a bowl of butter. Finishline somberly poured a cup of cider for Goldie and filled his own cup. The strange story cast a pall over the room. Despite the sun streaming through the windows, Goldie shivered.

"He wasn't happy about it," Barley admitted, "but it did save him money over the long run."

Finishline nodded. "Because he did not have to pay sales tax."

"Exactly. Even including the shipping costs it still worked out cheaper to use mail order parts."

The grave robbings halted (the Mayor continued) but soon after we spoke the gruesome packages began to arrive. Almost daily, secretive, furtive men would bring them to his door, or leave them with neighbors if there was no one at the castle to sign for them. Piece by piece, Lachtenslachter assembled his masterwork. Limbs were carefully matched for proportion, while the facial components—ears, eyes, nose—were chosen to give a pleasing appearance. Scalp, eyebrows, and lashes were created from the finest hair. Teeth were chosen that were free from cavities, and any skin with a trace of an old tattoo or piercing was rejected. Yet it was more than physical perfection that the Doctor sought. He believed that he was creating a being that was morally pure. An artificial man, brought to life from inanimate meat, would not be subject to hereditary vices, he claimed. Raised in a nurturing environment, educated to modern standards, his creation would be free of superstition, hypocrisy, and malice. Thus he set his goals high, perhaps too high, too lost in his dreams and carried away by his own ego to understand what he was doing. Until that dismal night when rain beat on the windows and lightning rent the air. That night when the creature cast aside its shrouds and rose from the operating table, when it focused its cold blue eyes upon Doctor Lachtenslachter, and the Doctor gazed back in horror as he realized what he had created.

"I am very much interested in this story you are telling us, Mayor Barley," explained Finishline. "You have my undivided attention. So I assure you it is not necessary to pause for dramatic effect as you are doing now."

"Tell us," added Goldie. "What did he create?"

Barley spread his hands in resignation. "We should have suspected. Indeed, it should have been obvious. Not only to

Doctor Lachtenslachter, but to any one of us. Where could those body parts have come from? And what sort of person did they come off of? It was during the war against the infidels. So many young soldiers going to the east, so few coming back alive."

The couple exchanged puzzled glances. They were about to question Barley, when comprehension struck both of them at the same time. Finishline's eyes grew wide. Goldie shrank back against her chair. "No," she whispered in abject dismay. "No, surely he didn't. How horrible."

"Yes," said Barley. "He created *a teenager.*"

Finishline grimaced. "Ouch." He accepted one of the plates of ham and steamed cabbage that Evelyn brought out. "That is a pretty tough blow for any man to take."

"It certainly was for Doctor Lachtenslachter," Barley agreed. "A teenager. Moody, sullen, sarcastic. Neglected his chores, played his guitar all hours of the night. Doctor Lachtenslachter didn't know how to handle him."

"No one knows how to deal with a teenager," said Goldie.

"True," said Barley. "But most parents are eased into it gradually. They get advice from their friends and their parents who have been there. Doctor Lachtenslachter had no help and no warning. He got the full impact of Eddie's personality right away. Words cannot describe the friction between those two. Even after Eddie left, the Doctor was never the same."

"He left?" Goldie looked around. "Where did he go?"

Barley exchanged looks with his wife. Evelyn was tight-lipped. She moved some plates around the table, avoiding the eyes of her guests. Barley sighed. "We were at fault, too," he said. "The village, I mean. It's a small place, and we should have been more supportive, more understanding. Perhaps things wouldn't have turned out the way they did."

"Nonsense, we had to do it," said Evelyn. "It was that guitar playing that drove us to it."

"Eddie got into the blues," explained Barley. "And we couldn't get away from it. He never stopped. Day and night, summer and fall, it was always the blues. It seemed that no matter where you went, you were bound to run into him, singing about how his woman done him wrong, or if it wasn't for bad luck he'd have no luck at all. You have no idea how depressing that stuff can be. Sure, we've all had our runs of bad luck and women who did us wrong ..."

"And men," said Evelyn.

"Men and women who did us wrong, but we don't sing about it all the time."

"Why couldn't he learn a nice polka instead?" asked Evelyn. "Something cheerful, instead of that dreary blues all the time. You can't even dance to it. He could have learned the accordion. Accordions are nice. Girls like accordion players."

"They do?" said Goldie

"My Uncle Walter played the accordion and he had girls flocking around him at the annual sheep shearers' ball. He could play and dance at the same time."

"Right. So this kid Eddie ..."

"The villagers drove him out of town," said Barley, regretfully. "I blame myself. I should have done more to try to stop them, but I ... well, I just didn't. We'd had a hailstorm, the crops had been damaged, and we were feeling pretty bad already. He was working on a new song—I think he called it the 'Lightning Bolt Blues'—and he was playing the same twelve bars over and over and, well, something just seemed to snap inside of us all. Before we knew it we had the torches lit and were chasing him through the forest. He never returned. A tragic fate awaited him."

"Yes, I can just imagine it." Goldie nodded. She could picture the scene in her mind. "He was cast out by society, driven from his home, rejected by those who should have loved him, penniless, despairing—it's obvious that there was only one thing he could have done."

"Exactly. He became a professional musician. And there are the stories, for it is said that he roams the mountains, forests, and bistros of Travaillia, a lonely, haunted figure, forced to survive by playing cheap gigs in smoky bars. Some even claim to have caught a glimpse of him, in the light from a candle stuck in a straw–covered Chianti bottle. And that," finished Barley, "is all that is known. Will you be wanting dessert?"

Although Evelyn promised the strudel had been freshly baked only the day before, Finishline and Goldie decided to skip it and went back out to their cart. They both paused to look at the castle. The sun was now overhead, streaking the stone walls with harsh light while putting the windows in deep shadow, like dark eyes in a flat, stern face. The chilling tale they had just heard infused the castle with an ominous atmosphere. Goldie found herself giving a little shiver at the sight of it, even inside her fur coat, and Finishline clamped his hat more firmly on his head. "Still," he reassured Goldie, "the guy sounds like he has the kind of skills we need, and I am certain that for a short amount of time we can tolerate any teenagers he might have, even if they are musicians. So we will have no cause to get in trouble, which we certainly want to avoid. Since we have come all this way, I suggest we finish the journey before this ice melts."

Goldie nodded and let Finishline help her back into the cart. He hitched the horse back to the cart, and the two visitors started up the road to the castle.

"It's a racehorse," said Andy. He was stating the obvious, he knew, but someone had to say something, and there was no sense trying to be clever until he and Doctor Lachtenslachter had some information to work with.

He had already decided he was going to help them. He couldn't explain why, although later he would turn the decision over in his mind. Perhaps he was pleased by the way they both spoke to him as an equal, instead of talking down to him as an adolescent, and that they didn't simply dismiss him or try to order him around. Perhaps he felt a bit sorry for them, the man in his worn suit, and the woman in the slight shabby fur coat. Perhaps he just liked the affectionate way they looked at each other. Whatever the reason, he made up his mind even before they stepped down from their cart.

"It is a racehorse," said Finishline. "A thoroughbred racehorse. This means he is descended from a long line of stallions that originated in Arabia. He is a three–year–old, which is a very good age for a racehorse to be. He has run sixteen races and finished in the money thirteen times and you will not find a better track record than that in all of Travaillia, for a three–year–old. This is a horse that has won a lot of potatoes for its previous owner and it is worth a good bit of scratch."

"Except that it's dead," said Andy, walking around the cart. "Correct me if I'm wrong, Mr. Finster, but isn't the market for dead horses kind of depressed right now?"

He tried to keep the enthusiasm out of his voice, but he was excited. He'd been hoping for another good project. With the pony out of the way, it didn't seem like the summer held much to do. He didn't have Eddie to pal around with this year, and since Eddie left, Doctor Lachtenslachter had been moody and hard to talk to.

He had tried to suggest, as subtly as he could, that the

Doctor make another try this summer, perhaps creating a teenage girl. He had even sent away for catalogs, but the high cost of the parts dismayed him. "These are a lot more expensive than the stuff we bought for Eddie."

"We were able to use military surplus," Lachtenslachter reminded him. "If you want to build a woman from parts you have to pay full retail. What are you planning to do with a teenage girl, Andy?"

"Nothing!" said Andy hastily. "Absolutely nothing, I swear it! I—um—just wanted to check the prices."

"That's just the construction costs. The pretty ones also tend to be high maintenance. The clothes cost more. And you have to buy them gifts and things."

"Call me Finishline, Andy," said Finishline, bringing his attention back to the topic at hand. "And yes, you are summing up the situation quite nicely. This racehorse, despite his many fine qualities, suffers from the drawback of being recently deceased. My ever-loving girlfriend, Goldie, and I both notice this quality the moment we clap our eyes on him. Thus we are able to buy him from the knackers at a very good price. And this is a very big advantage to us, because under normal circumstances Goldie and I do not have enough capital to buy a racehorse, and certainly not a champion thoroughbred three-year-old such as this one.

"But," continued Finishline. "Prior to the unfortunate demise of this fine animal we are talking to a guy who hears a story from a doll who is talking to a guy who plays in a blues joint (Here Finishline and Goldie exchanged uneasy glances, hoping that the mention of this would not strike a sore nerve with Lachtenslachter) and this story is that there is a Doctor in Barrenstock who can arrange things so that the rowboat ride across the River Styx is not necessarily a one-way trip. So Goldie and I invest almost our last bit of scratch to buy this racehorse from the knackers and cart him up here to you and now we are more than somewhat interested in hearing the Doctor tell us whether we are glomming onto a very good thing or if we are merely a couple of very big saps."

Doctor Lachtenslachter had also been walking around the cart all this time, examining the racehorse from every angle. He put on his spectacles and looked at it closely. Andy knew this meant he was thinking. Lachtenslachter didn't actually need spectacles, but he kept a pair anyway. He once explained to Andy, "If someone asks you a question, you can put your spectacles on and look at them. Or you can take them off and look at them. Either way, it gives you a moment to think before you answer. Also, if you point at someone with your finger, it's considered rude, but it's okay if you gesture toward them with your spectacles."

Andy pulled back more of the tarp, so all of the horse was visible. It lay on a bed of cracked ice. The ice was slowly melting, letting a steady trickle of water drip through cracks in the bottom of the cart. The horse lay on its side. The tail hung out the back of the cart. The ears were pressed against the front boards. The coat was still muddy and needed to be curried, but they could see the color was a deep, rich brown. It had black socks and a black blaze on the forehead. It looked very peaceful. A few flies buzzed around it. Periodically Lachtenslachter would poke at it.

Andy climbed on the cart to get a closer look at the legs. He brushed the ice away from one of the hooves. "What kind of shoe is this? I've never seen horseshoes like these."

"Racing plates," said Finishline. "They are made of steel instead of iron. They are very thin and light in weight."

"What was the cause of death?" asked Lachtenslachter. It was the first time he had spoken since he had come out to greet the visitors.

"A spike through the noggin, Doctor. It is driven by a rather large guy with a rather large mallet. This horse breaks his leg in a surprising accident—particularly so to because he is favored to win and because I have bet some money on this horse—and has to be put down."

"The leading horse slipped coming into the stretch," added Goldie. "It was a muddy track. The next horse ran into the first horse and another horse ran over them both. This one was second."

"Internal injuries?" Andy asked Lachtenslachter.

"Possibly. I'll have to do an examination, but that won't be a problem. Soft tissue heals more quickly than bones." Andy could already hear the enthusiasm in the Doctor's voice. They walked around it some more. Finishline and Goldie waited expectantly.

"We'll need a lot of blood," Andy said. "His blood has already deteriorated. I'll make a trip to the abattoir."

"I suggest we prepare plasma. He can make his own corpuscles once we regenerate the bone marrow. Until then we'll keep a breathing mask on him, using dephlogysticated air under pressure. You'll have to modify the pony mask to fit, Andy."

"I can do that."

"So you'll take the job?" said Goldie anxiously.

"Hmmm? Oh, yes. I don't see that it will present any major problems. The bones and muscles all seem to be intact. We'll replace any internal organs that may be damaged, check the connective tissue, fire up the cardio system, and reboot the brain. How much time do you have before you plan to race him again? I usually recommend a twenty-four hour burn-in period for the nervous system before you put him into action."

"We are hoping to run him in the Durk's Classic."

Lachtenslachter pursed his lips. "That's not much time."

"We're hoping very hard that you can help us," said Goldie. "The truth is, we must run the Roan Ranger in the Durk's Classic."

"The Roan Ranger?" asked Andy. He looked at the horse again, then looked down the drive to see if perhaps another cart with another dead horse was coming up.

"This horse is named the Roan Ranger."

"But it's a bay."

"We didn't name it, Andy."

"He can answer to the name of King Bruno of Omnia for all I care," said Finishline. "The important question is whether he can be made to run again."

"Not for the Durk's Classic," said Andy. "That broken leg will take a long time to heal. Isn't that right, Doctor Lachtenslachter?"

"I'm afraid my assistant is correct. Broken bones take many months to heal."

"Forget the leg," said Finishline. "This leg is past history. This leg is never going to heal so that the horse can run again. That is why they put down a horse with a broken leg to begin with."

Lachtenslachter exchanged looks with his assistant. Andy shrugged. "Then I don't see ..."

"We brought a replacement leg," said Goldie. She waited while Finishline pulled the tarp completely off the cart. Something long, slim, and dark brown lay buried in the cracked ice. Everyone moved to the back of the cart to get a better look at it. "In fact, there are two spare legs in there. I thought that instead of switching one leg, you might be better off switching both. Else the horse might be unbalanced or uncoordinated, or something like that."

"Quite right," said Lachtenslachter.

"Good thinking, sweetie," said Finishline. He squeezed her arm before turning back to the men. "These legs come from a horse call Toucan Play, who also is a very fine horse that has to be put down. In fact, Toucan Play is a very powerful starter, so we think that with Toucan Play's legs and the Roan Ranger's stamina, we have the makings of a very fast racehorse."

"We made sure the knacker was very careful when he cut off the legs," said Goldie. "He didn't scratch or scrape any bone. Even the tendons are almost untouched."

Doctor Lachtenslachter examined the spare legs through his spectacles, then took them off and examined the legs again, apparently comparing them to the legs still on the Roan Ranger. He put his spectacles back in his pocket and walked around the cart, one arm folded across his chest, the other hand rubbing his chin. Andy, Finishline, and Goldie stayed silent and let him think. Eventually he said, "All right. I can do it."

"Excellent!" said Andy.

"But does it have to race in the Durk's Classic? That's not very much time. Also, I would think that you'd want to start him out on something a little less challenging. Have you considered a turf race instead of a dirt track? I'm told they're easier on the horses' legs."

"He is already registered for the Durk's Classic, Doctor. And the truth is that myself and my ever-loving fiancée are more than somewhat short of potatoes at this time. We do not have the scratch to enter him in another race."

"The stable that owns him didn't remove him from the Durk's Classic," said Goldie, "or announce that their horse was put down. It's too late to get their registration fee back, so they don't care. The tipsters think the horse is recovering from an injury. The stable thinks we're going to enter another horse, and they're even going to let us run it under their colors. Like us, they're pretty angry at Waxroth."

"Waxroth?" Lachtenslachter's expression completely changed. He had started out by showing professional detachment, which was followed by a slowly growing enthusiasm. Suddenly a reluctance to continue showed on his face. He stepped away from the wagon. "Werner Waxroth?"

"Do you know him?"

"I know of him. The financier and fixer."

"We are indeed talking about the same person," said Finishline. "Unfortunately I owe more than a little money to

Werner Waxroth, and while Werner Waxroth is very generous about making short term loans at high interest rates, he is not the type of guy that a citizen wants to owe money to for very long. In fact, we have spoken of the matter just recently and he suggested to me that if I do not redeem my marker by the time the Durk's Classic is over he is likely to relocate my kneecaps to warmer climes."

"I am sympathetic," said Lachtenslachter, in a voice that indicated he was not sympathetic at all. "But I have a responsibility to Andy. Andy is not my apprentice. His family sends him here for the summer and he volunteers his assistance. His parents would be very upset if they thought I got him involved with persons of, shall we say, low character. The kind of people who resolve their differences with joints of lead pipe."

"Wait a minute," said Andy. He had also been building up a head of steam for the project, and he was dismayed to see that safety valves seemed to be opening and bleeding down the pressure. "Who is Werner Waxroth?"

"A bookmaker," said Finishline. "He accepts bets on horses."

"A crooked bookmaker," said Lachtenslachter. "And a gambler and a fixer. He manipulates the results of sporting events so he doesn't have to pay out on them. What's more, he uses his gains to finance other illegal activities. And to bribe officials to look the other way. Andy, it would be irresponsible of me to accept this project. I cannot do anything that might get you involved with hoodlums and gangsters."

"I am not happy about this myself," said Finishline. "I find it very distasteful to attract the attention of a person of low character. I much prefer to deal with honest citizens unless, of course, the results of the dishonesty are in my favor."

"Okay," said Andy. "So he's fixed a few races. Is that going to involve us?"

"He fixed more than just a few races, Andy. He fixes everything. Horse races, tournaments, games, sporting events, elections, teeth—everything that a man can bet on."

"Teeth? He fixes teeth? He's a dentist?"

"No," said Goldie. "He runs a pool on how many of his original teeth a man will still have when he dies."

"Well, I suppose people who want to gamble don't have to bet on sports events. They could just buy lottery tickets."

"He fixes the lottery."

"Okay, okay. Something else, then. People will bet on just

about anything. I've been told they even bet on dance marathons."

"Fixed."

"The annual Lower Styppewick Summer Faire Watermelon Eating Contest ..."

"Fixed."

"You're making this up, right?"

"Andy," said Lachtenslachter. "Did your school teach you about the war between Omnia and Draconia that took place when you were young?"

"The Ninety Day War? Sure."

"Fixed."

"Wow!"

"Well, he does not really fix the whole war," clarified Finishline. "Just the battles of Hellesfont, Ambergris, Green Lake, Jackson's Cove, Hill 23, The Fens, and Morgan's Reek."

"Okay," said Andy. "I can see you have a point." He wasn't really concerned about the problems of gamblers, or whether races were fixed or not. His parents didn't gamble and none of their friends did either, as far as he knew. But he realized that disparaging gambling in front of these two customers would not make for a good working relationship. Instead, he addressed Doctor Lachtenslachter. "The way I see it, there are two possibilities here. Either the Durk's Classic is not fixed, in which case we have nothing to worry about. Or the race really is fixed. In that case, if the Roan Ranger wins we'll be upsetting this gangster's plan. He'll lose money. So we'll really be fighting crime. We'll be doing a public service. I think we owe it to the people of Travaillia to thwart this man's scheme."

This was, of course, a stupid argument by any standard. While Finishline and Goldie, true to their gambling natures, managed to keep their faces expressionless, inwardly they were rolling their eyes. But Andy knew Doctor Lachtenslachter better than they did. Like himself, the Doctor was eager to take on a new project. Fitting a new pair of legs to a dead racehorse, then bringing it back to life, and doing it so that it could win a major race was a challenge he couldn't turn down. All Andy had to do was give him a way to rationalize it.

Lachtenslachter did not weaken immediately. He said, "Such men are dangerous. He might seek revenge. It will be a painful experience if I have to replace your kneecaps, Andy. It's hard to get a good fit."

"He does not always do kneecaps," said Finishline. "That is more like a figure of speech."

"Usually he breaks arms," said Goldie.

"He won't even know we're involved," said Andy. "We've been in far more danger from some of the creations here in the lab. Not to mention playing around with lightning and being threatened by lynch mobs. A gangster is a gangster. We know who this man Waxroth is, and we can prepare for him. In the lab, we're dealing with the unknown."

The two visitors were surprised, but Andy was not, when Lachtenslachter reflected on his words for a minute or so and then nodded agreement. But he also said, with an air of resignation, "Andy, in your school, were there any students who regularly got into trouble? And when it happened, did their parents say they were good kids who were led astray by bad companions?"

"We had a few of those, yes. Parents always say their kid fell in with bad companions."

"And when they mentioned the bad companions, did any of them give *you* significant looks?"

"I didn't notice. Come on, Doctor Lachtenslachter. Let's get this horse out of the sun and onto the slab."

"Very well. Finishline, bring your cart to the loading dock." Lachtenslachter started walking away. "Andy, make sure they fill out the admission forms in triplicate. Then take inventory of all our surgical supplies and make sure we have everything we need on hand before I start cutting. Mrs. Theis, you and Finishline may stay here at the castle if you prefer. I may have questions for you, and here will be more convenient than the village inn. The rooms are quite comfortable."

"Thank you," said Goldie.

"We will need some help to get this animal out of the cart and onto your operating table, Doc," said Finishline. "It is pretty heavy."

"We have a sling set up for that," said Andy. "You and I can do it. The villagers don't like to get involved in our experiments."

Lachtenslachter began walking back to the castle door. "I'll notify the maids to prepare your rooms and the cook to set two extra places for dinner. Andy will tell the stable boy to take care of your cart horse." He looked at the sky. It was still clear and blue. "The sun will be down by the time we're completely set up. I prefer not to operate, nor conduct an examination, in dim light, so I'll examine the horse tomorrow morning. If it looks all right I can attach the new legs tomorrow afternoon."

"Good," said Finishline.

Lachtenslachter was still looking at the sky. "We need to hope and trust that we'll have an electrical storm when we're ready for it. Fortunately they are common, here in the mountains, at this time of year." He frowned. "However, we also have a time constraint with this race coming up, so it will be best to have the horse ready as quickly as possible. It will need some time to recover, and you'll need some training time, I'm sure."

"We do."

"We will discuss it after dinner and work out a schedule. I'll introduce you to my niece. She loves horses. Oh, and by the way, meals are informal here—no need to dress for dinner. Have I forgotten anything?" He stuck his hands in the pockets of his lab coat and looked pensive. "No, I think that's it for tonight." He reached the big double door to the main hall and put his hand on the knob.

"Oh, there's just one more thing," he tossed back to Finishline and Goldie. "You'll need to find a new brain for this horse."

CHAPTER THREE

Andy stood on the roof of the castle, where Doctor Lachtenslachter had set up a rain gauge, an anemometer for measuring wind speed, a windsock for direction, a thermometer, a barometer, and a few other instruments. He was disappointed. There was only a little wind, and the atmospheric pressure remained high. Nothing indicated a storm was coming. He logged the readings in a small notebook, which he then tucked into a pocket of his lab coat. He descended from the roof via an iron ladder to a third floor balcony. Entering the castle through the French doors, he made his way to the laboratory, where Doctor Lachtenslachter was checking an inventory list against a shelf of bottled eyeballs, and noting which ones needed to be restocked. He nodded to Andy and exchanged the clipboard for the notebook. "What does it look like out there?"

"Sunny and clear, I'm afraid."

"It's just as well, I suppose. We're not yet ready for a storm. And when the animal is ready, we will simply have to trust that a storm will come along in good time." He clapped Andy on the shoulder. "We have to accept the things we cannot change. I read that in a fortune cookie last week, so it must be true." Lachtenslachter picked up a femur and examined it distastefully. He had purchased it from a South Seas supplier who supposedly obtained it from a cannibal tribe. He tossed it to Andy. "Ship this back to the dealer, Andy, and demand a refund. This one has teeth marks on it."

Andy caught the bone with one hand. "No problem. My fortune cookie last week said the day was good for making new friends."

"I always thought that Friday night was the best night for making new friends. Saturday night is date night, so everyone is already coupled off."

"I'll keep that in mind, Doctor Lachtenslachter, if I meet someone I want to date."

The Doctor looked at his young assistant thoughtfully. "Andy, you've been doing good work here. I don't know if I've told you that enough."

"You have, Doctor Lachtenslachter. But thanks anyway."

"On the night that we throw the power switch and bring this racehorse to life, would you like to be the one to scream, 'Life! Give my creation life!'?"

Andy was pleased. He knew that Lachtenslachter loved to do the "Life, give my creation life" routine, so this implied a great deal of approval. He said, "Thanks, Doctor Lachtenslachter. That will be great."

"You're welcome. Now, I've purchased a few limelights for the laboratory. Limelights are the type of lights they use in theaters. We want to set them up so they will throw spooky, dramatic shadows around the room."

"Got it."

"And make sure that our lab coats have plenty of fresh bloodstains on them."

"Okay."

"It's important to put on a good show for the clients, Andy. I know I've told you this before, but it's worth repeating."

"Right."

"Science is not like sorcery. Its methods are not concealed by arcane symbols and secret rituals. Science is at its best when done in an atmosphere of open inquiry. No special gift or talent is required. Anyone can do what we do. All it takes is hard study, a logical mind, and a desire to seek the truth."

"I understand."

"That is why it is not enough to simply present the public with the results of our studies. We must keep them informed, if they are at all interested, of every step in the process. We must light a candle for them and lead them down the path of knowledge, so they can experience for themselves the *thrill of scientific discovery!*"

"Scientific discovery. Right. Got it, Doctor Lachtenslachter."

"But remember not to give them any of the math. Math only puts them to sleep."

"No math. Okay."

The clients in question chose that moment to enter the lab. They did not look cheerful. They did not look terribly unhappy, mind you, for both Finishline and Goldie were inclined to put their best face forward, but Andy thought he detected a general air of dejection that hung over them. He said, "No luck?"

"We are not able to find a suitable brain."

Lachtenslachter looked surprised and said so. "Is it that

hard to get a head? Surely the knackers' yards and the tanning factories have scores of skulls available."

"There's plenty of heads," explained Goldie. "But they all have holes in them. That's the way horses are put out of their misery. Someone puts a spike against the forehead and hammers it in with a big mallet. It's supposed to be quick and painless."

"Although how they determine that this method is painless to the horse is something I do not know. Perhaps they assume it is painless because the horses do not sue for malpractice afterward."

"Well, ask the knackers not to spike the next one," said Lachtenslachter reasonably. "Work horses collapse in the street all the time. Surely they would be willing, for a token payment, to set one aside for you. Then they could end its suffering by some other method."

"My parents are always complaining that the apothecary on our street makes his pills big enough to choke a horse," added Andy. "We can get one of those pills and toss it down the horse's throat."

"It is somewhat more complicated than that, Andy," said Finishline. He put his thumbs in his waistcoat pocket and drummed his fingers against his stomach. "Doc, are you absolutely certain the existing brain cannot be repaired? Perhaps you can just sort of fill in the hole and patch over it?"

"It is, as you yourself just said, somewhat more complicated than that. Come, let me show you my notes on the brain." Lachtenslachter led them to another table. Andy followed them. The table held a thick stack of foolscap, held down with a brass paperweight. Each page was covered with dense handwriting. The edge of the table was lined with bottles of ink in different colors. Scattered across the tabletop were large sheets of vellum. All of these held hand–drawn and carefully labeled diagrams of something that looked like a head of cauliflower that had been left in the field past the first frost date. "The brain," explained Lachtenslachter. "I have been studying its functions for many years. It is the brain that controls the body. It is the brain that is responsible for thought and speech. Yes, I know, for many years it was thought that the heart was the center of consciousness. And there are those who still hold the view that the spleen is responsible for emotion. The brain was merely thought to be useless fat. But in these more enlightened times we know that the brain actually has a function." Unconsciously, Doctor Lachtenslachter adopted a lecturing tone, as though he were addressing a classroom of medical students. Finishline and Goldie, neither of whom had done well in school, automatically looked around the room to see if there was another student whose notes they could borrow.

"I'm kind of disappointed to hear that," said Goldie, turning her attention back to the Doctor. "I still like to think the heart is the center of emotions. It's more romantic. Isn't it, Finishline?"

"Sure," said Finishline. He looked over the drawings. "So you are saying that the horse absolutely has to have a new brain, Doc? It needs a new brain to race?"

"Without a doubt. The old brain was damaged beyond repair when the horse was put down. Here, look." Lachtenslachter riffled through the vellum drawings until he found the one he wanted. He slid it across the table to where his two clients could see it clearly. "I'll use a human brain as an example. This sketch shows each section of the brain that corresponds to certain skills. For a human brain, there are different sections for speaking, hearing, logic, verbal skills, and reading the backs of cereal boxes in the morning. Men and women's brains are slightly different." Lachtenslachter pulled up another drawing. "For example, this part of the brain is used for thinking about shoes. It tends to be much larger in women than in men."

Goldie looked past his hand. "What is this area here?"

"That is the part of the brain that women use for thinking about sex."

She compared it with the second drawing. "Where is the area that men use to think about sex?"

"They don't have one. At least, no one has found it. The current theory is that when a man sees a woman, the nerve impulses go directly from his eyeballs to his waist without his brain getting involved at all."

"Ah. That explains a lot."

Finishline said, "If we can turn the discussion back to horses ..."

"Your horse was damaged in the area that controls motor skills. Without a new brain, it won't be able to walk."

"We don't really want it to walk."

"It has to walk before it can run."

"Okay, Doctor, I hear you loud and clear. I understand that the horse needs a new brain." Finishline took off his hat and rubbed his temples. "Doc, for two days we have been trying to get a brain from a winning racehorse. That is because Goldie and I instinctively have the feeling that to rebuild a winning racehorse, you must have parts from a winning racehorse." The gambler shook his head. "And what you are telling us, Doctor, confirms our own fears. A racehorse is a highly competitive animal. A good racehorse is born with a will to win. They are bred from winners generation after generation. Then, from the time they are little horses, they are trained to run faster than the horse next to them. Every time they are on the track they are encouraged to beat the other horses. Now, if your theory is correct, and all that instinct and training is lodged in the horse's brain, then we need a brain that is fully stocked with a desire to beat the competition. If you put the brain of a draft horse in the skull of that racehorse that's lying on the slab, we are just going to end up with a draft horse with spindly legs."

"So we need a brain that came out of another racehorse," said Andy.

"But that is something we are not able to get. We are not able to buy a cheap racehorse and harvest the brain, because Goldie and I do not have the scratch to buy even a very cheap racehorse, even if there was such a thing as a good cheap racehorse, which there is not."

"If we could buy a good racehorse," Goldie said, "We would just leave the brain inside it and race that horse."

"Well, I'm sorry that your brilliant plan has come to naught," said Lachtenslachter. Andy could see that he really was sorry. The Doctor had taken a liking to his new clients. "But the brain we have is beyond repair. You can take my word on this. I've seen a lot of brains. You won't be able to run this horse without a new brain. I can splice up a lot of the severed nerves. I can get him breathing again, and perhaps even up on his feet. But he'll never be able to do much more than take children for rides at the county fair. All I can suggest is that you go back to the track and hope for another accident in the next few days."

Finishline exchanged resigned looks with Goldie. "I suppose that is the end of the story. We have a shortage in the brain department. In any case, what we really need is the brain of a *winning* racehorse, and that is totally beyond our means."

"No, it isn't," said Andy. "I know where we can get one."

"No," said Lachtenslachter quickly. "I know what you're thinking, Andy. It's out of the question."

"MacGool," said Andy. "He has what we need."

Lachtenslachter collected his drawings and started shuffling them together. "It doesn't matter. He'll never sell it."

"Who?" said Goldie, "are we talking about?"

"Are we talking about Doctor MacGool?" asked Finishline. "The veterinarian?"

"You know him?"

"He is the track vet at Geht Downs. It is his job to examine the horses to make sure they are not doped to make them run faster."

"So it probably isn't a good idea to use a brain that came from him," said Goldie.

"It will be inside of the horse," said Andy. "He won't be able to see it. And he has the preserved brain of a winning racehorse. He showed it to me."

"Doctor MacGool?" said Finishline. "Why is he preserving a horse's brain?"

"He sells parts," said Lachtenslachter. "As a side line from his veterinary business. Rather poor quality parts, I'm afraid, and his prices are way out of line. I certainly would not rely on any brain that came from him."

"He's a collector, too. He has top of the line stuff," said Andy. "Doctor Lachtenslachter doesn't like to deal with him because he is a competitor."

"A mere dabbler in science. A rank amateur. He's hardly a competitor. On occasion I have felt sorry for him and given him a few pointers. Not that he ever acknowledged them."

"He wrote a paper that was published in a veterinary journal. He said he invented a surgical technique that he actually learned from Doctor Lachtenslachter."

"A small matter." Lachtenslachter shrugged. "Let him have his little claim to fame."

"Anyway, he has his private collection that he doesn't sell. It's pretty cool. Parts from famous people and animals. He has the larynx from Jean Chablis, the famous opera singer. And the palate of James Entrecote, the food critic. He has the tail of Sassie, a famous collie that pushed her owner, a boy named Tommy, into a well. And he has a small selection of horses' heads. Not many, but he does have a racehorse."

"Which one?" said Finishline quickly.

"Something called "Elastic Band.""

Finishline looked thoughtful. Goldie pursed her pretty lips and gave a long, low whistle.

"I guess you've heard of him, then."

"Elastic Band," said Finishline. "His sire is Bandleader, who is well known for setting a record at the Viaduct that holds to this day. His dam is Rubber Ducky, a fast starter and a champion on the short course. Elastic Band, in his heyday, is a very fast horse indeed."

"None of which matters to us," said Lachtenslachter. "Because MacGool is not going to sell. You know that, Andy. He has a pancreas that I've been trying to buy for months. A beautiful specimen," he explained, turning to Finishline and Goldie. "Really top notch. I offered him top price for it, more than it is worth, really, but he won't sell parts out of his collection. The very definition of a collector is that they collect, they don't sell. He loves that little museum of his. He shows it off to anyone that visits him."

"I'm not suggesting we buy it, Doctor Lachetenslachter," said Andy. "We just—ah—make use of it."

"You mean steal it," said Goldie.

"Well, maybe. Sort of. It's not like it's guarded or anything."

He looked nervously at Doctor Lachtenslachter. Lachtenslachter was genuinely shocked, and said so. "Andy, I'm surprised at you! How could you suggest such a thing? I already set aside my doubts about letting you associate with gamblers, and that is only because gambling is not illegal in this country. But what you're proposing is outright theft! I couldn't possibly countenance such a thing. What would your parents say?"

"Doctor Lachtenslachter," said Andy patiently. "We use stolen parts all the time. How do you think the grave robbers get them? By robbing graves. We even robbed a few ourselves, remember? Before the villagers came down on us."

"That's completely different!" Lachtenslachter's voice rose half an octave. "Grave robbing is an ancient and honorable profession!"

"It is?" said Andy

"It is?" said Finishline and Goldie together.

"Well actually, no, it isn't. Good point. But the people who had those parts were dead. The parts didn't actually belong to anyone, anymore. Not anyone living. This horse brain we're talking about belongs to someone."

"Someone who bought it from someone else who took it off a dead body. It's the same thing we do."

"No, it isn't. A person owns himself, and when he dies his body is consigned to the earth. But people own horses and the carcass still has value. It's like stealing horsemeat from a butcher's shop."

"The butcher's shops don't sell horses' brains. They sell the meat and the hides. Maybe in some countries they sell calves' brains. But a horse's head just goes into the garbage. You know that, Doctor Lachtenslachter. Dead horses are always being abandoned in the streets. The city has to haul them away." Andy was thinking fast now. "Once the body has died, it's just clay. Ashes to ashes, dust to dust, and all that. It returns to the soil, right? Right? So what MacGool really has is a piece of dirt that belongs to whoever owned the scrapheap. The city or the county or whatever. So technically he received stolen property. Except that there's no reason to worry about, because at this point it's really just a piece of dirt."

Lachtenslachter sighed. "When small children want something," he told Finishline and Goldie, "they whine and cry and stamp their feet. Then when they become teenagers, they learn to reason with you. And frankly, it's not much of an improvement."

"He is making a good point," said Finishline. "I myself see this brain as being somewhat in the public domain."

Andy could tell that Lachtenslachter was weakening. "Listen, Doctor Lachtenslachter, I won't steal the brain outright. When I take Elastic Band's brain, I'll switch it with the brain from this horse."

"What difference will that make?"

"It makes us even. Doctor MacGool wants the brain of a champion racehorse for his collection." Andy patted the carcass of the Roan Ranger. "*This* has the brain of a champion racehorse. Patch it up a bit and MacGool won't know the difference."

"*I'll* know the difference." But Lachtenslachter hesitated before he said this.

"*He'll* be satisfied with it. He won't know it's damaged. He's never going to put it into action."

"This is a much prettier brain," said Goldie.

Lachtenslachter looked at her. "How do you know? You've never seen the other brain."

"A woman has a feel for these things. This horse's brain has style. It has éclat." Goldie put a finger to her cheek and looked at the Roan Ranger the way a woman might look at a credenza in an antique store window. "Yes, if I were to pick a brain to display around the house, this is the brain I'd choose."

"Think of that perfectly good brain over there going to waste," said Finishline. "Confined to a glass jar, locked away in a stuffy museum, when it can be galloping across golden sunlit meadows, drinking from cool mountain streams, enjoying the fresh air, winning races, and making children smile. It is enough to break a man's heart."

"All right!" said Lachtenslachter. "All right, that's enough. I give in. We'll switch brains. I'll take this brain out and repair the damage as best I can." He looked out the window, where the sun was still high, but the shadows were lengthening. "We need to allow extra time before the race. I need to give the new brain a physical before I put it in. We'd better switch them tonight. Andy, can you be ready?"

"I'm ready right now," Andy assured him.

The Vice-Director of Marketing placed a brown bottle firmly in Cordy's hand. He twisted the bottle until he judged the position was correct. "Perfect," he told the girl. "Always hold it like this. You want to be sure the label is showing. Practice picking them up until you naturally hold it like this."

The girl held the beer as instructed for a moment, then turned it around to look at the label, then turned it again so the it faced away from her. "Right," she said, trying to show enthusiasm. She was dressed in riding clothes. Not hunting clothes, nor casual riding clothes, but clothes such as a jockey would wear. White silk jodhpurs, a bright blue silk blouse with a large white number four on the back, and thin black boots. Her hair was tucked under a black cap with a short brim. Her cheeks were pink and the skin of her face was wind burned, revealing that she had spent most of the morning outdoors.

The Marketing Manager looked at the bottle critically. He took it back from her. "Excuse me, Cordy." He reached into a tooled leather case and rooted around until he came up with a plant mister. Gently, he sprayed the bottle until beads of water were hanging on the sides. This created the illusion that water was condensing on the cold glass. It gave the impression of a cool and refreshing beverage, although the bottle was, in fact, quite warm. He handed it back to Cordy. Dutifully, she grasped it so the label was facing away from her, trying to make the action seem natural.

"Okay, let's say the grandstand is in that direction," said the Marketing Manager. "Hold the bottle up and smile."

Cordy did so, revealing a dazzling display of even white

teeth in a pert, lightly tanned face.

"Widen your eyes."

Cordy lifted her eyebrows to present a wide-eyed, innocent look.

"Excellent," said the marketing guy. "Rod?"

Rod would be announcing the race now known as the Durk's Classic. For years it had been called the Durk's Cup, but two years ago the people in the marketing department at the Durk's Brewery decided the race had been run for enough years to be called a classic. Or perhaps they just thought that a race called the Durk's Classic sounded classier. Rod looked up from his script and intoned. "When you're galloping your stallion down the home stretch and every ounce of weight counts, a winning jockey can't get filled up. That's why champions like Corduroy Brown prefer Durk's Light. Durk's Light has the fine flavor you've come to expect from Durk's, but with less calories."

"Fewer calories," said Cordy.

"What?"

"Durk's Light has fewer calories. Not less calories. It's *less* filling because it has *fewer* calories."

Ron checked his script. "This says less calories."

"Stick to the script," said the Marketing Manager. "That's the way the advertising people want it. So Rod does his introduction, then you raise the bottle toward the grandstand and say …"

"Fine flavor, fewer calories."

"Less calories."

"But it's not right," Cordy protested. "It makes me sound dumb."

The Marketing Manager beamed. "Exactly! It's supposed to make you sound a little dumb. The customers relate to you better that way."

"Why? Don't smart people drink beer?"

"Of course they do. Just not Durk's. Anyway, Cordy, we never try to market a product to smart people. No one does. There are not enough of them to make it worthwhile. Now try it again."

"Fine flavor, less calories," said Cordy, smiling through gritted teeth.

"Work on it a bit tonight. Now, we'll be optimistic and assume you're going to win the race. So you'll go straight to the Winner's Circle to dismount. Otherwise, just parade your horse before the grandstand until the winning horse exits the Winner's Circle, then ride in. You can wait around because the Durk's Classic is the last race on the program. But whatever happens you stay on the horse. You ride in wearing the Durk's Brewery colors ..."

"Wait," said Cordy. "I'll be riding Jumping Jack Flask in the Durk's Classic. I'll be wearing his stable's colors."

"As you come off the track and pass in front of the judges' booth, one of our spokesmodels will hand you a blouse in the Durk's colors. Pull it on over your riding colors. She'll also hand you a hot towel. Wipe the dirt off your face and hands, and give it back to her."

"Wash my face. Got it."

"Then you get to the Winner's Circle. More of our spokesmodels will be there. A bunch of really beautiful girls. Act like you know these girls and they're your friends."

"Are you going to have any good-looking boys there?"

"The guys will have average looks, so more of the customers will identify with them. We want to give men the impression that beautiful girls like nothing better than to hang around racetracks with guys who drink our beer."

"But surely everyone knows that already?"

Sarcasm was lost on the Marketing Manager. "It's important to remind them." He consulted his notes. "Now, one of the models will uncork a bottle of Durk's Light and hand it up to you ..."

"Will there be a problem with that? The track regulations don't allow alcoholic beverages beyond the fence. They're pretty strict about it."

"Good question," the Marketing Manager said approvingly. "We've taken care of that." He crossed in front of her, took two bottles from a table, and brought them back. "These two bottles are identical." He showed her the first bottle. "This is a normal bottle of Durk's Light, a delicious beer with a clean, fresh taste, carefully crafted by master brewers from the finest ingredients, using a traditional recipe." He showed her the other bottle. "This looks like a bottle of Durk's Light, but actually all it contains is plain water. We've made the racetrack authorities aware of what we'll be doing." He took a sip from the bottle and frowned. "No, wait a minute. *This* one contains plain water." He sipped the other bottle and frowned again. "Damn. Rod, which one of these holds the light beer?"

"The light beer has bubbles."

"Really? That's interesting." He tasted both bottles again,

then held one out to Cordy. "You take this bottle of water ..."

"Wait a minute. You didn't know that beer has bubbles?"

"I'm not a drinking man, myself."

"But you sell beer!"

"I never like to research a product too thoroughly before I design a marketing campaign. It interferes with the creative process. Now, you grab the beer—that is—the water ..."

"With the label out."

"With the label out—very good—can you do a head toss?"

"A what?"

"That thing that girls do where they toss their hair so it swirls around them?"

"Sure, but my hair is pretty short. It doesn't swirl much."

"Let's see."

Cordy took off her riding cap, allowing her brown hair to puff out. She tossed her head. The Marketing Manager examined her critically. "No, leave your cap on. Never mind the head toss. So you take the bottle and hold it up and you smile and say ..."

Inwardly, Cordy sighed. Outwardly, she held up the bottle, put on her best smile, and said, "Fine flavor, less calories."

The town of Farlong was not large. Certainly there were many other cities in Travaillia that were much larger. It was big enough, however, that the people of Barrenstock and the surrounding countryside referred to it as "the city". The racetrack brought in visitors, and also had a rather nice fairground. The city boasted a respectable public library, and a park where the King himself rode not long ago. In Farlong's central square, right in front of City Hall, was a large fountain decorated with statues of frolicking sea nymphs. Periodically a small group of high-minded citizens would gather together to protest the nude statues, demanding that they either be covered up or replaced with more demure images. For several hundred years the mayors of Farlong had used these protests as a measure of their ability to rule the city. They figured that if the inhabitants had nothing more important to complain about than a few nude statues, things must be going pretty well.

Andy, Finishline, and Goldie sat in a small restaurant about a block away from MacGool's house, a place with nine square tables set with thin cloths, thick crockery, and pewter spoons. The air was filled with the scent of fresh baked bread and boiled mutton. A sideboard held a roasted joint, a ham, several chickens, and the remains of a goose. Finishline and Goldie were eating a fragrant dish that combined boiled tripe with garlic, red peppers, onions, and spiced butter. It was the cheapest thing on the menu. In Travallia, and in fact all of the surrounding countries, tripe was invariably the cheapest thing on any menu, but Andy had never seen anyone actually ask for it before. Finishline and Goldie seemed to order it automatically.

Andy had eaten dinner before they left the castle, so he was just having a second dessert of cherries with a brandy cream sauce. They all sat at a table near a window, one that gave them a view of the street. Because of other buildings in the way, they could only see the roof of MacGool's house. Finishline and Goldie kept throwing it nervous glances. Had even a single light come on in the upper level, they would have canceled the evening's excursion. But it remained dark.

"MacGool's house has only two floors," Andy explained. "But a very big attic. The first floor is his surgery. He also has his library there. The second floor is where he lives, with his bedroom and sitting room. The kitchen is in the basement. The attic is where he keeps his collection."

"How do you figure on getting in there, Andy?"

"Climb the drainpipe, in through the roof vent."

Finishline looked at him dubiously. "This is not going to turn into one of those scenarios where the drainpipe breaks loose from the wall and sways about in a comically alarming manner while Goldie and I run about beneath it, trying to catch you, is it?"

"Oh no. It's a good, solid drainpipe. The house is pretty new."

Finishline ate a spoonful of tripe while he thought. "It seems too easy. Why is it that every thief in the city does not try the same thing?"

"I think they all have. I know he's caught them at least twice. The bottom two floors have barred windows. The attic is solidly locked off from the rest of the house. When thieves get in, they strike a light, and find themselves in a room full of dead animal parts, many of them with eyeballs, staring at them from glass jars. It totally freaks them out. A couple of them just started screaming and those were the ones he caught. MacGool thinks it's pretty funny. Actually, I think it's pretty funny myself."

"It freaks me out just to think about it," said Goldie. "I can tell this man has a whimsical sense of humor."

"He's not really a bad guy. I'd feel bad about doing this if it was something really valuable. But it's not like there are a bunch of other collectors out there bidding up the price of dead animal organs. He's not really losing anything."

"Just do not get distracted yourself," said Finishline. "Do not scream. It will be difficult to explain your presence if he hears a noise and decides to investigate."

"I'm not the screaming type. He won't hear anything. He'll be downstairs, playing dominoes with Doctor Lachtenslachter."

"The sitting room will be right beneath you," Goldie pointed out.

"They don't play in the sitting room. They play in the library."

"That is another point of which I am curious," said Finishline. "For I am given to understand that our Doctor Lachtenslachter does not care a great deal for our veterinary acquaintance. Yet, if I am interpreting the situation correctly, he comes to town every week or so to play dominoes and otherwise exchange pleasantries. This requires some explanation."

"Well, they're rivals, sort of. They're not enemies. Beside, when you're doing the kind of stuff that Doctor Lachtenslachter does, you want to talk about it to someone. He talks to me, of course, but I think he gets tired of that. Doctor MacGool is really the only other person in Travaillia who can appreciate what we do. So Doctor Lachtenslachter can't resist telling him about his latest breakthrough, even if he thinks MacGool might steal his ideas again." Andy finished his cherries and licked the spoon. A waitress came around to light candles. Outside it had grown dark. He checked that both of the adults had put down their spoons. "Are we finished? Let's go."

Finishline left some coins on the table. He sauntered out the door with an overstated display of nonchalance. Goldie linked her arm into his.

"We should move quickly," Andy told them. "The game doesn't last that long. Doctor Lachenslachter said he would try to drag it out tonight, to give us more time, but still."

"Just stay with us," said Finishline. "Moving too fast attracts the attention of the coppers. Furthermore, a man alone attracts the attention of the coppers. And a running teenager really attracts the attention of the coppers. But a man and a woman together, out for an evening stroll, do not ring any alarm bells inside the head of a copper."

Andy cut back his pace to maintain only a small distance in front of them. He carried a simple burlap bag. The top was tied off with a piece of rope, and the other end of the rope tied into a loop, so that he could sling the bag over his shoulder. He reached the corner across from MacGool's house. It had a lamp post. He stood under it, rocking back and forth on the balls of his feet, until Finishline and Goldie caught up with him.

"And there it is," Andy told them. A stout clay drainpipe, about four inches in diameter, ran up the side of MacGool's building. It was attached to the stone wall with cast iron brackets. It certainly looked sturdy enough. "This won't take me but a few minutes. You can keep watch here."

Goldie looked nervously up and down the street. She wore smoked glasses and a black scarf over her golden hair, which Andy suspected was her idea of a disguise.

"Andy, are you sure you know what you're doing? Finishline and I have met our share of shady characters, including a certain number of thieves. I'm not trying to put you down, Andy, but you don't really strike me as a second story man. Have you ever cased this joint? How do you know what's on that roof?"

"Doctor MacGool took me up there once. I was helping him install lightning rods, like the ones Doctor Lachtenslachter and I put up on the castle. He showed me the whole building."

"That clears up the mystery for me," said Finishline. "Until now I am conjuring up visions of your youth misspent in diamond heists and philandering."

"MacGool is okay, pretty much. As long as you're not bargaining with him. He's overcharged us plenty of times. Any loss he takes on the brain he'll earn back from us in trade."

Finishline looked back over his shoulder. There is no way to do this casually but he gave it his best shot. He stuck his head around the corner and scanned that street also. For a man who was trying not to arouse suspicion, it was the most suspicious-looking action Andy had ever seen. He was glad Finishline was not going into MacGool's house with him.

Both streets were empty. Most of the people in town were still at their evening meals, and in fact the smoke from a hundred stoves was blowing down from the rooftops, making the murky darkness even murkier. "No one is on the street," he said. "I suggest that if you still want to do this, it is a good idea to do it very soon. Like right now, for instance. And do it quickly."

"I'm going," said Andy. "Keep watch while I'm inside."

"Right," said Goldie. "If we see someone coming, we'll ... what? What should we do?"

"I don't know. I'm new at this. Just keep watch."

Andy was, of course, a young man in good shape, and he had plenty of experience climbing around the roof of Doctor Lachtenslachter's castle, installing and maintaining the equipment there. Still, Finishline, whose own pipe–climbing days were over, was surprised at how quickly Andy reached the tiled roof. He said as much to Goldie.

"I'm more interested in this keeping watch thing we're supposed to be doing," Goldie told him. She pulled down her smoked glasses and looked over them. "What are we watching for? What do we do if we see a copper? We can't call out to Andy, since that would attract the attention of the copper. We can't signal him by throwing pebbles at a window, because that would only alert MacGool."

"I suppose that if MacGool comes out of his house we can engage him in conversation so he doesn't look up. If a copper comes by and seems to be paying undue attention to the house, then you and I start an argument so as to distract him."

"There he goes," said Goldie, looking up. They watched Andy lift up a trapdoor, and disappear into the attic. "And that's that."

CHAPTER FOUR

Andy entered a room that was not quite as black as pitch, but certainly as dark as, say, really good bakers' chocolate. He hung by his fingertips, dangling in the air with his feet just above table level, not wanting to let go blindly and send a rack of fragile glass jars crashing to the floor. The attic had shuttered vents at each end, under the eaves. These, plus the open trapdoor, let in only a dim glow of moonlight, but eventually Andy's eyes adapted to it, and he was able to drop to the floor without incident. He peered around the attic, wondering if he could do the job in near darkness. A light might be seen through one of the vents. A candle, even a wax candle, would also leave an odor that would take a while to dissipate, possibly tipping off MacGool that an intruder had been here. Eventually he decided to risk the light. Carefully setting the burlap bag on the floor, he removed a stub of a wax candle from one pocket and his tinder box from the other. A few strikes with a flint enabled him to light his candle. A warm glow suffused the room, golden light flickering and reflecting from a myriad of glass jars and glass-fronted cases. And that allowed him to discover a problem.

The problem was not the eyes. A hundred or so eyes did indeed stare at him silently from their jars of preserving fluid. As he had explained to Finishline, the effect had been unnerving in the extreme to those trespassers who had come upon them unexpectedly. Several petty thieves, apparently of the superstitious sort, admitted they still had nightmares several months after their encounter, and at least one refused to eat eggs fried sunny-side up, declining any food that seemed to be looking at him from the plate. But Andy had been here before, and the eyeballs held no fear for him.

Nor did the organs present a problem to him. They floated peacefully in their jars of formalin and alcohol. It is true that the sight of a pickled kidney might turn the stomach of someone who has only encountered them fully cooked inside a steak-and-kidney pie, and a human lung is particularly revolting if it came from a smoker. But since he started assisting Doctor Lachtenslachter, Andy had seen just about every organ there was, and gore held no fear for him. Besides, he had seen MacGool's collection before.

No, the problem was with the labels.

Andy had been up to MacGool's museum twice before. Both times he had been accompanied by, of course, Doctor MacGool. Andy hadn't paid much attention to the labels, except to note that everything on display had one. He hadn't needed to look at the labels because MacGool was there to explain, in the exhaustive detail of a man enthused about his hobby, just what each display was, where it was from, and why this particular specimen was the best of its kind.

Andy held the candle flame close to a label on a glass jar, so close the flame left a smear of soot on the glass. He frowned and rubbed it off. He moved the candle to another label. Like the first, it was neatly lettered in India ink. Also like the first label, it was completely unreadable. As were most of the rest of the labels in the museum. They were in a foreign language, and one Andy had never seen before.

He looked up through the trapdoor. The moon was almost overhead, moving across the opening. He wondered how much time he had. Lachtenslachter and MacGool's evening visit did not last particularly long. It wasn't absolutely necessary for Lachtenslachter to keep MacGool downstairs, but it helped. He put his free hand on a cabinet and drummed his fingers while he thought. MacGool had several thousand organs packed into the attic room. But only a small percentage was brains, and not all of the labels used the strange alphabet. Notations in Greek, Latin, and Travaillian were mixed in. If the organ came from a famous person, then the celebrity's name was included on the label, along with the date of death. Those names were in Travaillian. The dates were in Roman numerals. Andy remembered that the brains were near the center of the attic. If the name of the horse, Elastic Band, was on the label, he could find it easily enough. Also the racehorse had died not too long ago. MacGool had only recently added it to his collection. So if the date was included on the label, that would narrow down the search.

He knelt on the floor next to the burlap bag, and carefully set the candle on the edge of a table, so the light would shine on the bag from above. He untied the drawstring and let the edges of the bag fall around the object inside. It was a heavy glass specimen jar, similar to the type of jar MacGool used in his museum. In fact, it was a jar MacGool had used, for it had formerly housed a duodenum that Lachtenslachter had purchased from MacGool, including the pyloric valve, for which he had to pay extra. Lachtenslachter always insisted on installing new valves when he swapped out abdominal parts. "They only add a little to the total cost and the reliability is much improved," he told Andy. The jar now held the damaged brain of the Roan Ranger, delicately extracted and packed by Lachtenslachter that afternoon.

Andy put the jar under his arm, picked up the candle, and stood up slowly. He moved into the center of the room, where three shelves were arranged in a U-shape. The shelves extended almost to the roof, with specimen jars set edge to edge. These racks held MacGool's brains, both humans and animals. As Andy brought the candle around in a slow circle, he couldn't help feeling a little envious. MacGool really did have some good brains here. Andy reminded himself that the brains Lachtenslachter chose had to be functional. MacGool mostly collected them to display. Sure, they looked hot, but could they really perform when you put them to the test?

A sudden draft blew out his candle. Andy made a "tch" sound of annoyance. He squatted to the floor, put down the candle and the Roan Ranger's brain, and felt in his pocket for his tinderbox. This time the tinder didn't want to catch the sparks from the flint right away. He had two lucifer matches for back-up, but they produced a sulfurous smoke that would linger for hours. He didn't want to use them unless it was absolutely necessary. It took nearly a minute to get the candle lit again, although to Andy, who got more and more nervous as time went by, it seemed like an hour. When he finally got another light he left his jar on the floor and used his free hand to shield the flame. Bringing it close to the shelves, he spotted the jar he wanted. It was undoubtedly a horse's brain, and though the label was a mixture of different alphabets, he was able make out one neat set of block letters—ELAS—and then the candle went out again.

Never mind, Andy told himself. He had found the jar he wanted and he knew where it was. He decided to dispense with the candle, which could attract attention anyway, and finish the job by moonlight. He held the Roan Ranger's brain up to the shelf and compared it with the jar on the shelf, turning it around in his hands so the glass reflected the slight glow from the open trapdoor. He could not see any difference between the two jars, or the two brains inside. He replaced the jar on the shelf with the Roan Ranger's brain. Returning to his burlap sack, he extracted a small jar of either and an artist's paintbrush. He painted the ether onto the label, where it dissolved the glue without smearing the ink. Peeling off the label, he waved it in the air a few times to give the ether a chance to evaporate. Then he took a small pot of fresh glue from the bag, removed the stopper, and used it to paste the label onto the substitute jar. While he was doing this the thought crossed his mind that the glue he was using may have been boiled down from horses' hooves, and that irony might be in play here.

He stood back and inspected his work. In the faint white light the rows of jars appeared to be untouched. Satisfied, Andy packed everything up in the burlap sack, slung it over his shoulder, and boosted himself up through the trapdoor and onto the roof. He was feeling rather pleased with the night's adventure, like one of the gentleman burglars from a story in a penny magazine, and he gave a jaunty wave to Goldie and Finishline when he saw them below. Finishline gave him a sour look and made a patting down motion with his hand.

Andy immediately dropped to his stomach. The sky was clear and the moon was quite bright. He would have been easily seen by anyone who happened to look up. Staying flat against the roof, he squirmed forward until his eyes were barely over the edge and looked down.

A constable was walking up the street toward MacGool's house, swinging his billy club in a complicated pattern. He also watched Finishline and Goldie, who were talking to each other. They stopped and nodded pleasantly to him as he went past. He gave them a suspicious look, but kept going and eventually faded from sight.

Andy gave a mental sigh of relief. He raised himself up to his knees so he could crawl over to the drainpipe. Finishline saw him and made the "get down" motion again.

This time it was an old woman, carrying a string bag of potatoes in one hand, with her other hand clamped, claw like, over the top of an umbrella. Andy wondered where she was buying produce at this time of night. She walked slowly, arthritically, but she had a smile for Goldie. Finishline took her sack and guided her across the street. It took some time, but she too faded into the night and Andy stood up.

And got back down again when he heard a crying baby. A man in laborer's clothes came by with a squalling infant in his arms. "Teething," he called to Goldie. "He's been like this all day. I thought I'd take him for a walk, give my wife a chance to rest."

"Mmm mm," said Goldie, with a fixed smile. She didn't move. The man was surprised, expecting that she, like every other woman he met on the street, would want to take a look at the baby. But he shrugged it off and continued on his way.

This time Andy did not bother to get up. In short order there came a street sweeper, a news peddler, a deliveryman, and another constable. Then a courier in a tight uniform and pillbox hat ran past, a letter clutched in his hand. He was followed by a group of six people in evening dress, then another group of four, apparently on their way to the theater. A group of musicians in black clothes hurried past, instrument cases under their arms. The two constables came running back up the street, chasing a miscreant. And then there was another crowd of theatergoers, a dozen or more, headed in the opposite direction from the first group, toward Restaurant Row, perhaps after getting out of an earlier show. Followed by an elderly man taking his evening constitutional, moving ever so slowly down the street, stopping frequently to lean on his cane. Finishline and Goldie watched every step. Finishline tipped his hat as the man walked past. Goldie gritted her teeth. Andy began to wish he'd brought a book to read.

He waited. Down below, his partners in crime peered up and down the streets. Goldie stayed in lookout position while Finishline walked around to look in to alleys and doorways. Finally, Finishline gave Andy the high sign. Andy nodded down to him, swung a leg out over the edge of the roof, and started the climb down the drainpipe.

He'd hardly got started when all at once, people started pouring out of the buildings. Andy froze in place. Finishline and Goldie looked around in shock as hundreds of men, women, and children seemingly appeared out of nowhere to fill the sidewalks. From the dark end of the street Andy heard the sudden, ominous pounding of drums. The drumming got closer. Then a fanfare of trumpets added to the noise, the crowd began cheering, and an entire thirty piece brass band burst into song. In full uniform, buttons shining in the lamplight, they marched down the street, led by three majorettes and followed by a baton corps. They passed directly beneath Andy to the tune of "Oh, Won't You Take Me to the Bower." Fortunately no one looked up.

Some of the children ran to follow the band, but the rest of the crowd broke up immediately after they passed and disappeared back into their homes. Andy's arms were trembling with the effort of holding himself to the drainpipe. The brain jar seemed to be growing heavier by the second. He gave Finishline a questioning look. Finishline, completely baffled by this time, just shrugged.

Andy quickly climbed down. He rolled his shoulders to get the kinks out of the muscles while Finishline and Goldie came across the street to meet him. "I am beginning to think that Farlong is not such a toddling town," Finishline told him.

"What was that all about?" Goldie demanded.

"I don't know," said Andy. "I'm not usually here during the summer. I'd have come into town more often if I'd known I was missing out on all this action. Anyway, I've got the brain."

Naturally everyone had to have a look at it, even though Finishline and Goldie couldn't tell one brain from another. Andy also wanted to see it in good light. It went without saying that it wasn't a good idea for Andy to open his sack right across the street from MacGool's house, so they carried it a block away and around a corner and stood under a street lamp. Andy took the specimen jar out of the sack and each member of the trio took a turn holding the brain up to the light and admiring it, in the same way that people who can't tell a good horse from a bad one will nonetheless make complimentary remarks when circumstances call for them. "To one such as myself, this looks like a very fast brain," said Finishline. Goldie and Andy agreed that it was the brain of a winner.

"I guess," said Andy, when they had all satisfied their curiosity, "that it probably isn't a good idea to carry this back to Doctor MacGool's house. I'll leave it with you while I check to see if Doctor Lachtenslachter is still there."

He put the bottle of brains back in the sack and handed it to Finishline, who cradled it gingerly in his arms like a bachelor who has been given an infant nephew to hold. Andy retraced his steps to MacGool's house and hammered with the knocker. When the servant let him into the foyer, he requested Doctor Lachtenslachter. He was a bit surprised when MacGool himself came to greet him.

"Oh hello, Andy." MacGool was older than Lachtenslachter. His hair had more white in it, and there was just a trace of stiffness in his walk. "Doctor Lachtenslachter left already, I'm afraid. He asked me to tell you that he'd meet you back at home."

"Yes, I thought that might be the case. I'm a little late. Thanks anyway, Doctor."

MacGool looked out beyond Andy. "What a nice night. That's what I like about this side of town. The streets are so quiet and peaceful in the evenings. Nothing ever happens out there."

"Um, right." Andy tried to keep his face expressionless. "So ... um ... Doctor Lachtenslachter said he was going right back to Barrenstock, did he?"

"You just missed him, Andy. He left only a few minutes ago. But no, he's not going right back. He said he had an errand to run before he went home. You might still be able to catch him."

"Here in Farlong? Do you know where he went?"

"He didn't say. But of course, I think we can both guess where he went." MacGool gave Andy a sympathetic smile. "I'm pretty sure he went to see Eddie."

The Blue Tune was a half hour walk from Restaurant Row, located in the basement of the building whose chief attraction was its cheap rent. To enter you had to take three steps down, and many of the club's patrons considered this an emotional as well as a physical journey. It was dark and it was dingy, as its owners felt a blues club should be. The waitresses were skinny, with long black hair and an overabundance of eye shadow. The tables and chairs were old and scarred. Yellowed paper peeled from the walls. The Blue Tune gave the impression it had been around forever, and that many of Travaillia's most famous performers had started their careers there. That was, in fact, true of the original Blue Tune, which had closed several years before. This one had been open for only eight months and bore no connection to the original. The owners spent many hours steaming the wallpaper to get it to peel just right.

It was also rather smoky. Not because its patrons smoked all that much, but because the ventilation was poor. On this point the owners were rather disappointed in their regular customers. They thought people who spent their evenings hanging out in blues clubs should smoke heavily. It bothered them no end that their customers frequently asked to have another window opened.

Only a few candles lit the interior, partly to create the desired dim atmosphere, mostly just to save on candles. The Blue Tune was not a high profit operation.

Eddie loved the place. He knew the managers and one of them had helped him get his first paying gig, farther south in a town called Desdemona. He always included the Blue Tune in his swing through Farlong, and they always had a slot for him, either solo or as part of the band. When he wasn't playing he found a table in front of the stage and chatted with the club regulars. Tonight he put his guitar to one side, and let one of them, a hot girl, pull her chair around to his side of the table. She was wearing a maroon dress that was tight in all the right places, which on this girl meant it was tight everywhere. Except in areas where it didn't exist at all, such as the neckline.

She leaned forward, giving Eddie an excellent view of her cleavage, and slid her hand inside his shirt. "Oooo, Eddie. You have so many scars."

Eddie took her hand and moved it up to his heart. "The scars you can see are not important. It's the scars inside that will never heal."

"Ooo," said the girl. "You're so sensitive." A tear welled up in one eye. "And yet, so strong, to endure the pain and loneliness."

That was the great thing about being a musician. Aside from being able to sleep all day and stay up all night drinking, there were the babes. If Eddie had been a customer, coming to this nightclub to meet girls, he would have had to chat up this babe, buy her a drink and then another, and hope she showed enough interest in him to justify asking her out. But merely because Eddie went up on stage, the girls asked *him* out and even bought him drinks. It was strange, but the way Eddie figured it, he didn't make the rules. Girls made rules for dating and guys just had to play the game the best they knew how.

There was no doubt his good looks also helped a lot in that department. Some girls said that Eddie had the body and face of a young god. They were absolutely correct. Lachtenslachter had modeled him after a statue of Adonis he'd bought at an antique store. He had the statue delivered to his laboratory so he could work from it. Eddie's arms, legs, shoulders, and chest were all well–muscled and perfectly proportioned according to classical ideals of the male figure. His stomach was flat, his back was straight. Eddie had features that were fine without being delicate, a firm jaw, even teeth, an aquiline nose, high cheekbones. They were all connected by a network of scars. Not ugly scars, mind you.

Lachtenslachter's reputation as an expert surgeon was well deserved. The scars on Eddie's face were very thin scars, most no thicker than a hair. They were also very faint, although in bright daylight they gave the impression that Eddie was looking at you through a fishnet stocking. There was nothing exactly scary about the scars. They were just a little disconcerting until you got used to them. For daytime gigs, Eddie concealed them with stage makeup.

But in candlelight you couldn't see the scars at all, another reason Eddie liked the Blue Tune. And candlelight gave gold flecks to the girl's green eyes. Eddie stared directly into them, over the straw-covered Chianti bottle, ignoring her cleavage for the time being. "It's the music that keeps me going, that has always kept me going, through the nights of loneliness and despair. Nothing can keep me down as long as I have my music ... and ..." He paused and clutched her hand more tightly, as though struggling to express his feelings. "Someone beside me, someone who understands."

"I understand, Eddie," the girl said earnestly.

"I know you do. If only I could ... damn!"

"What?" The girl looked around.

"Someone I don't want to see." Eddie watched an older man with gray hair enter the club, look around, and go to the bar. "But he's going to see me anyway." He gave the girl a peck on the cheek and scooted her away from the table. "Something just came up. Listen, stick around and we'll talk some more after my next set, okay?"

The green-eyed girl looked a little baffled by the sudden change in tone, but nodded and went back to her own table. "He has such a beautiful soul," Eddie heard her tell her girlfriends. He wondered if Lachtenslachter's eyes had adjusted to the darkness yet. If not, perhaps Eddie could slip away. But no, he still had another set to play. And his father was already coming over.

Lachtenslachter was carrying a cocktail glass very carefully, in the manner of a man who doesn't often drink in bars and is not used to paying nightclub prices for alcohol. He set the drink down at a table across from Eddie, set himself down in a chair next to the drink, looked around and said, "So. Eddie. Nice place you're working in."

The Blue Tune was not supposed to be a nice place to be in. It was meant to be a depressing place, a place that would attract people who wanted to drink a lot so they would forget someone, and listen to torch songs to remind them of who they wanted to forget. This hadn't happened yet but the owners still had hopes. Still, Eddie did not want to have a family discussion in the Blue Tune. He didn't want to have a family discussion anywhere, but especially in a place where he worked. Lachtenslachter, he felt, was intruding on his space. He growled in the back of his throat, then said, "What are you doing here?"

"What?" said Lachtenslachter. "Can't a man go out and have a drink? I was in town, I was nearby, I heard you were playing, I thought I'd stop in and see how you were getting on. And here you are. So, how are you getting on?"

"Fine. And having established that, you can leave now."

"I thought I'd stick around awhile and hear you play. The doorman said you were going to do another set."

"You've heard me play. You've heard me sing. You don't like my music."

"Maybe it sounds different in a place like this," said Lachtenslachter. "The acoustics are probably different here. They're ... um ... smokier." Eddie glared at him. Lachtenslachter avoided meeting his eyes by looking around some more. "This is probably a good crowd for a weeknight, right? Interesting people, you get here. Did they come to see you? Ah, there's a man with trumpet. Does he play with you?"

"Blind Man Harper. No, he doesn't play anymore. He just hangs out here. He blew his lips out years ago."

"Really?" Lachtenslachter brightened, feeling he was on familiar territory. "He needs a new pair of lips? I can sew on new lips. Ask him if he wants new lips. I can get him a very good deal."

"What he wants right now is to drink and be left alone. And I feel the same way."

Lachtenslachter pretended not to notice this hint. He continued to look around the room. "All these different guitars." He pointed to a half dozen display guitars, some of them signed, that hung on the walls. "All different sizes. I didn't know they made that many different kinds of guitars."

"They've been customized," said Eddie. "Musicians have different sized fingers and different length arms. So the necks and fret boards are adjusted to fit the guitarist."

"Does that help them play better?"

"Nope, not at all. Okay, maybe a little. It's mostly just guitar wanking, though."

"Custom fret boards for different fingers," Lachtenslachter mused. He shook his head. "No, it's the wrong way to approach the problem. Standardize the fret boards instead, and customize the fingers."

"What!"

"Do you need new fingers, Eddie? How are they holding up? I could adjust them. Or even add extra fingers, so you could play more strings."

"What?"

"I've got it! Heavy duty fingernails, so you don't have to use a pick."

"Oh, for God's sake." Eddie slapped an open palm on the table. "Dad, you really have no idea what you sound like, do you? Do yourself and everyone else a favor and try and look beyond the operating table once in a while. A man is more than a collection of parts."

"I merely offered a suggestion. I'm just trying to be helpful."

"I don't need help! I'm just fine, doing what I want to do. I'm not your patient anymore. I'm a professional musician."

"A professional musician?" Lachtenslachter waved his arm, a gesture than encompassed the dim room. "You call this a profession? A doctor, a lawyer, that's a profession." Even as he said this, Lachtenslachter mentally bit his tongue. The subject was one of his hot buttons, and he knew that he should have let it pass. But once again he had responded in the same old way.

"Yes, I call it a profession," Eddie shot back. It was one of his hot buttons, too. "What do you call what you're doing, an obsession? Stringing together dead body parts in the name of science?"

"Don't belittle *me*, Eddie. It was science that created you, the culmination of years of research." Lachtenslachter's voice rose. "It is I, and I alone, who holds the secret of creating life."

"Yeah? What about that Scotsman? The one who created a sheep?"

"He used a mix! They're never as good as when you make them from scratch."

"Oh right. I'm impressed. Dad, I've got news for you. Any woman can create life." Eddie let his eyes flick to the green-eyed girl, still sitting on the other side of the room. "They do it all the time, and without fancy laboratories. Hell, you have to take special precautions so that they *don't* create life. All a woman needs is the right guy. That, and maybe a few drinks to loosen her up first."

"Obsolete technology! It's painful, messy, there's no quality control ..."

They both stopped when the waitress came over, taking a moment to sit back in their chairs and seethe at each other. But the waitress directed Eddie's attention to the edge of the stage, where a drummer and bass player were looking anxious and making pointing-at-the-clock motions. Although the nearest clock was in the town square, six blocks away, Eddie knew what they meant. He stood abruptly. "That's my cue to go on, Dad. Don't feel like you have to stay."

"I guess I need to be getting back anyway." Lachtenslachter stood also. He tried to think of something conciliatory to say, but Eddie had already turned his back. The doorman held the door open for him. Lachtenslachter went up the three steps. The music started just as he reached street level. He lingered outside, long enough to listen to the first song. It was the Lightning Bolt Blues. Lachtenslachter pulled up his collar and walked into the darkness.

CHAPTER FIVE

Andy didn't ask Lachtenslachter any questions when he got back to Barrenstock. He always knew when the doctor was thinking about Eddie, because he tended to mope around the castle and not say much. However, he brightened up considerably when Andy showed him the replacement brain, and when, early the next day, storm clouds appeared over the mountains, he got right to work. Lachtenslachter assigned most of the support work to Andy, watching from the background while Andy sewed on the new legs and attached the tendons. They also re-expanded the lungs, using a device Lachtenslachter had designed from a blacksmith's bellows. Finishline made another trip to the city to buy horse's blood from the knackers, after the Doctor decided that whole blood would let the horse recover more quickly. They bubbled dephlogysticated air through the blood and circulated it through the horse's arteries, until the gray skin took on a healthier tone. It was late afternoon, and the sky was fully overcast by the time they got back to the brain. However, Lachtenslachter already had the top of the skull off, so it didn't take much time. He inserted the brain, spliced in the nervous system, and pronounced it a perfect fit. The top of the skull was fitted in place and held down with silver pins, then the scalp was stitched together with nearly invisible sutures. Lachtenslachter recessed the electrodes to just beneath the surface of the skin. Once the horse was brought to life, Goldie would glue horse hair over them and dye it to match the rest of the Roan Ranger, so they would be barely visible. Deedee helped out by making crayon drawings to decorate the new horse's stall.

Andy was expecting a pretty calm resurrection this time. The approaching storm didn't look like it would be particularly powerful, and he and Lachtenslachter had been through the procedure many times before. Nonetheless, Lachtenslachter insisted that they put on a good show for the clients. So Andy polished up the surgical instruments before they started cutting, they both wore scrubs and surgical masks while they worked, and they used a lot of medical jargon when they spoke to each other. Andy kept the glue and duct tape out of sight. Lachtenslachter thought Finishline and Goldie would get bored and leave after a while. Andy understood how much their futures depended on the Roan Ranger. The couple stuck around for the whole operation.

Lachtenslachter set a few bottles of sparkling wine to chill in a tub of spring water, so they could drink a celebratory toast when the horse came back to life. "I'd really like to set things up so a sudden draft blows out all the lights just at the right moment, except for a few candles to backlight the creature just as it is rising. I've seen similar things done on stage. It's a very dramatic effect. I don't know where we can hide a wind machine, though."

"It's too bad we probably will never get the Saint Elmo's Fire again," said Andy. "That looked totally cool."

"That was a bit more destructive than I'd like." They talked some more about possible ways to dramatize future projects, but eventually agreed that nothing more could be done for this one. So they connected the copper cables, set up the iron rods, and prepared for a bolt of lightning.

Nature was slow in cooperating. The storm took its time getting there. Periodically Andy would climb up on the roof to survey the sky, although truthfully he could see just as well from the windows. There were flashes of light in the mountain passes and he could hear the distant rumbles, but this storm had a very Zen attitude. It insisted on contemplating every movement. He only hoped it didn't fade away before it reached the castle.

There was nothing to do but wait. Finishline and Goldie were quiet at dinner, lost in their own thoughts, which were mostly along the lines of what was going to happen to them if this didn't work. Finishline wished he had already started growing a beard in case he had to go into hiding and Goldie wondered how she would look as a brunette. She rather thought she remembered that someone told her there were excellent career opportunities overseas and considered that perhaps she and Finishline should investigate them. Andy and Lachtenslachter talked between themselves about the technical details of the resurrection. Deedee talked about her pony.

After dinner they got up a game of cards, but Finishline and Goldie were too distracted to play well. They kept standing up and going to the windows, watching the dark mass of clouds slowly coming closer, blotting out the stars as it moved in. Doctor Lachtenslachter suggested they get some rest. Andy offered to keep watch, and wake the others up when the storm hit.

"I am not feeling tired at this particular time" said Finishline. He had a printed broadsheet with him, that he had made pencil marks on. "So I am staying up to study this racing form, as I see there are some good investment possibilities coming up."

"I'm also too nervous to sleep," said Goldie. "Come on, Deedee. I'll put you to bed."

In fact, they both ended up dozing off in their chairs—nervous energy only lasts so long and leaves you exhausted when it runs out—and Andy had to wake them both up when thunder started crashing around the castle. He brought them to the operating room, where Lachtenslachter was dressed in a long white surgical gown. Andy had already opened the ceiling trap and run up the lightning rods. The thunder and lightning woke Deedee, who came down the stairs trailing her nightdress. Lachtenslachter sent her downstairs to unlock the front door.

"Why?" Goldie asked him. "Why do you want to unlock the front door?"

"Um, in case some of the villagers decide to drop by. For a cup of tea."

"In the middle of the night? In a thunderstorm?"

"Right," said Andy hurriedly. "They take their tea seriously in Barrenstock. You never know when they might throw a tea party." Goldie gave him a skeptical look but did not pursue the matter. Finishline just stared moodily at the horse.

The resurrection proceeded to go like clockwork. Lachtenslachter threw the heavy T-switch that connected the copper cables to the apparatus on the roof. Only a few minutes later a bolt of lightning struck one of the rods. The horse twitched spasmodically as the muscles contracted. The instrument dials jumped to position. Lachtenslachter disconnected the T-switch. The dials remained steady, indicating a flow of electrical fluid. He placed his stethoscope on the animal's chest. "Heart's going," he reported after a moment.

"Do we need to defibrillate?" said Andy. They could give it a small shock with electricity from a Leyden jar if they needed to.

"No, it's a nice, steady beat."

"Yes, I feel it. I've got a pulse."

The Roan Ranger's chest began rising and falling. Andy waited until he got the nod from Lachtenslachter, then disconnected the breathing mask. Respiration stayed normal. Lachtenslachter gave him a congratulatory smile.

"It is not moving," said Finishline worriedly. He had remained quiet up to this time.

"Don't rush it," said Lachtenslachter. "We'll give it a few minutes to stabilize, then we'll try to get it up on its feet."

"We need it to ..." Finishline's words were drowned out by a peal of thunder. "... do us any good if it is in a coma." He stepped to the operating table and poked the horse in the side.

The horse suddenly opened cold gray eyes. Finishline sucked in his breath and stepped backwards. Lachtenslachter leaned over the horse's head. "Pupils slightly dilated," he murmured to Andy. "Possibly from concussion." The horse shuddered along the length of its body, then lay still.

Goldie looked inquiringly at Lachtenslachter. "Patience," he advised. "Give it a minute."

The horse shuddered again. The tail twitched. With a sudden convulsive heave, it turned over and rose to its knees. The ears flicked and it gave a deep, rasping cough.

"Get ready," Lachtenslachter told Andy.

The horse pushed up on its front legs. They wobbled a little, then steadied. It lowered its head.

"Now," said Lachtenslachter.

"Life!" screamed Andy. "Give my creation life!"

The rain increased, hard drops that rattled on the tin of the trapdoor. A tremendous sheet of lightning lit up the laboratory. It was just the sort of dramatic effect Lachtenslachter had been hoping for. The lightning was followed immediately by thunder, a heavy BOOM that penetrated the thick castle walls with ease, filling their ears with a deep basso profundo that counterpointed Andy's maniacal cry. Startled, the horse rose convulsively to its feet. The sheets dropped away from the dark brown coat. The limelights cast it in sharp relief, showing every muscle that rippled beneath its skin. It swung its head, casting its eyes into every corner of the room, looking at each of the four inhabitants without a trace of fear or nervousness. The lips curled away from the large, strong teeth, and it gave out a disdainful wicker. It looked every inch a thoroughbred.

Goldie's eyes were filled with rapture. She put her arms around Finishline. "He's beautiful," she said. Finishline could only nod.

Andy leaned his head toward Lachtenslachter. "How did I sound?" he whispered.

"Fine." Lachtenslachter stripped off his gloves. "Fine, Andy. Very good."

"My voice didn't crack, did it?"

"No, it was fine."

Andy looked to Finishline. For a moment he was certain he could see a glint in the gambler's eyes, as though a stream of gold coins were cascading behind his pupils. He decided it was just a reflection of the lamp light. Finishline moved toward the operating table in a slow, gentle, sleepwalker's daze. "The Durk's Classic," he murmured dreamily. "A five thousand crown purse. The Belljar Stakes. Fifteen thousand crowns."

"The Cravat Cup," said Goldie, coming up behind him. She had the same faraway expression and the same dreamy voice.

Finishline took her hand. "Fifty thousand crowns."

"I'll need a new dress for Cravat Opening Day."

"You have it, baby. This horse is our ticket to the big time." With his free hand Finishline reached into his pocket and came out with a lump of sugar. Palm open, he raised it to the horse as if offering a chalice of sacramental wine to the God of Short Odds. "Here you go," he said reverently. "This is going to be the start of something beautiful."

The horse went crazy.

It reared back with a furious whinny, front feet pawing at the air. Then it came down so hard chips of marble flew off the operating table. Finishline jerked his arm back just in time to avoid having it crushed by the slashing hooves. The horse's eyes were no longer calm and cold. They radiated pure fire and anger. It jumped off the operating table, its shoes throwing sparks when they hit the slate floor, and crashed into a cabinet of chemicals. The cabinet went down. Glass bottles shattered on the floor, sending up clouds of fine white powder. The horse reared again.

"Prepare a sedative!" said Lachtenslachter quickly. He was still calm. Andy ran to get a syringe. Lachtenslachter tried to get around the horse, to a shelf that contained tranquillizers. The horse turned toward him and snapped its teeth. Lachtenslachter jumped back but the horse snagged a fold of his surgical gown, tearing off a large piece. The Doctor dove under the operating table.

Finishline and Goldie were still standing together, stunned

at the sudden turn of events and the unexpected ferociousness of the animal they had purchased. When it lowered its head and glared at them, it took them a moment to realize it was about to attack again. When they did, Finishline pushed Goldie away. "Get down, honey!" She dove under the operating table with Lachtenslachter. Finishline ran across the room, with the horse right behind him. He turned suddenly and let the horse crash into the wall. A shelf of books came down on top of it. The horse shook them off and charged again. Finishline ducked behind a cabinet. The horse turned and kicked, shattering the cabinet door with its rear hooves. Glass and books spilled onto the floor.

"What the hell is wrong with him!" the gambler yelled.

"I don't know," Lachtenslachter yelled back. "Andy!"

"I've got it!" Andy screwed a needle into a syringe and reached into the tranquillizer cabinet. "Which one!" The horse was running furiously around the room.

"Aqua nepenthe. No! Stay away from the horse. It's too dangerous. Roll it over here."

Andy rolled the bottle across the floor. When he saw Lachtenslachter reach out and snag it, he followed by sliding the syringe across the floor also. Lachtenslachter quickly filled it. But when he started to crawl out from under the table, the horse attacked again. A pounding hoof caught his sleeve as he pulled his arms back under the table. Another hoof reduced the syringe to glass powder. Goldie shrieked and put the table between her and the horse. It reared up and struck the table with its front hooves again, cracking the marble.

"Doctor Lachtenslachter" yelled Andy. "The mezzanine! Get upstairs!"

He pointed to the ladder. Lachtenslachter saw what he meant. He backed out from under the table, away from the horse, and pushed Goldie toward the ladder. He gave her a push on her shapely bottom to get her started, then followed her up to the narrow landing that ran around the operating room. The horse turned its attention to Finishline again. The gambler was attempting to shelter between some more shelves, but a second ladder leaned against the wall. Finishline reached it in three jumps. He swarmed up it and flopped onto the mezzanine just in time for the horse to destroy the ladder with two well-placed kicks.

That left only Andy on the ground floor, and the horse was between him and the remaining ladder. Andy didn't hesitate. He grabbed one of the copper cables, which were still hanging from the lightning rods, and began climbing hand over hand. He almost made it.

Immediately the hair on his arms rose, reminding him that the storm has not yet abated and there was still plenty of static electricity in the air. The cables were still connected to the lightning rods. But since the alternative was to stay at floor level with a thousand pounds of trampling horse, he continued. Lachtenslachter watched him anxiously. He pulled himself up to mezzanine level and began swinging on the cables, aiming himself toward the mezzanine.

"Give me your hand!" called Lachtenslachter, extending his own arm. Andy didn't hesitate. He jumped from the cable to the mezzanine rail. Four feet of blue spark followed him, shocking him into paralysis, but Finishline and Lachtenslachter caught his arms and pulled him over the railing. He sat down with his back to the wall, waiting for the white noise in his head to subside. Eventually he realized that someone was speaking to him.

It was Goldie. "Are you all right?"

"Well, I'll never be depressed again." Andy looked at his hands. They both had a line of blisters across the palms. "Yeah, I'm fine." Finishline and Lachtenslachter helped him stand up. He looked over the railing, along with the three adults. The horse was standing in the middle of the operating room now, glaring up at them. Occasionally it snorted and pawed the ground with a front hoof.

"I didn't know that horses snorted and pawed the ground when they got angry," said Andy. "I thought that only bulls did that."

"Apparently we have a brain from a racehorse with a very bad temper," said Goldie. "It happens sometimes. Race horses can be very high strung."

"I do not think so," said Finishline. "Elastic Band is a famous racehorse. Generally if a famous horse is a kicker or a biter, you hear about it. They make bad starts and lose races. The top jockeys will not ride them. Word gets around."

"It might be in pain," said Lachtenslachter. "Perhaps we didn't close a suture properly. That could make it irritable. Or it could be hungry. Its stomach is empty right now. I know when I get hungry I tend to get short-tempered."

"I am not seeing an irritated horse down there," said Finishline. "I am seeing a crazy loco horse down there. I watch horses all the time. This is not a horse with the jitters. This is a horse such that if it is hired to play the lead role in a stage production of The Demon Horse from Hell, it will not need direction."

"In any case, I'll need to examine it again before I can make a diagnosis. Clearly there is some important factor that I missed."

"Examine him?" said Goldie. "How?"

"I'll have to sedate it, of course. Andy, how are you feeling?"

"Just fine."

"Is there any way you can get a rope around its neck?"

"He needs more than a rope," said Finishline. "He needs a straitjacket."

"We have plenty of rope in the stables," said Andy. "I should have had a halter ready, to lead it out. I don't know why I didn't think of it. Anyway, I'll go onto the roof, climb down the outside wall, and get a rope and halter."

Lachtenslachter looked out the window. It was completely black outside, and although the brunt of the storm had passed, raindrops were still streaking the glass. "It's too dark and slippery to climb on the roof. Wait until the rain stops and the sun comes up. It will be safer in daylight. We can stay up here a few hours."

"Sure," said Finishline. "It is not like I will be able to sleep for thinking about the money we lost."

"Maybe the horse will go to sleep," said Goldie. "The rest of the lamps might burn down."

"I filled them this evening," said Andy. "They'll burn for a while yet." He frowned as he watched the horse prick its ears.

A slight scraping noise sounded from the operating room door. From their vantage point on the mezzanine, none of the humans could hear it, but down on the operating room floor, the horse picked up the sound readily. It turned to watch the door, hostility emanating from every pore.

When the people on the mezzanine saw the horse turn its head, they too focused their attentions on the door handle. Its polished brass gleamed in the lamplight, so they could easily, if uneasily, watch it turn.

"Who could it be at this hour?" muttered Lachtenslachter, thinking that this would be an opportune time for a few villagers with pitchforks to show up. His mind was clearly not working at its best, because there was only one possible answer and Andy voiced it a split second later.

"Deedee," he yelled. "Stay away!"

The door slipped open and the girl, carrying a candle holder in one hand, slipped inside. A broad smile lit her face when she saw the stallion. "Horsie!" she said happily. She let go of the door. It closed on the hem of her long flannel nightdress.

Andy was already running around the mezzanine. "No, Deedee! Go back!" The others also began shouting at her, which meant that all Deedee heard was a cacophony of voices, so she couldn't understand any of them. She put up a tiny hand and beckoned to the horse.

Andy reached the end of the mezzanine and looked down. The horse lowered its head. It fixed its eyes on Deedee and walked toward her with slow, ponderous steps. To Andy it looked like some beast of the forest stalking its prey. Each clang of the steel shoes on the stone floor rang like a knell of doom. "Run away, Deedee! Go back to bed, now! Deedee, go outside and close the door!"

Deedee ignored him. Her eyes were fixed on the half-ton animal that was coming toward her. She gently lowered the candle to the floor, then waved to the horse with both hands. "Come here, horsie."

Andy swung his legs over the mezzanine railing. A cabinet stood in front of him, about four feet away and ten feet below mezzanine level. Lachtenslachter saw him. "Andy! Stop! You can't jump!"

Andy jumped. He landed on the cabinet flat-flooted, hard enough to crack the glass front, both feet hitting the top with a single, heavy thunk. For a moment he teetered, wind milling his arms, trying to keep his balance. The cabinet rocked beneath him. Then it went over with a crash. Andy hit the floor on his back and lay still.

Deedee saw him fall. Alarmed, she forgot the horse and tried to run to him. But her nightdress, still caught in the door, pulled her legs from under her. She fell to her knees and, unable to stand up again, leaned back into a sitting position. She saw Andy raise his head, and realized for the first time that the adults were shouting something at her. A gray shadow blotted out the lamplight. She looked up. The horse loomed over her. A troubled expression crossed her face.

Andy was stunned, but he was still conscious. He rolled onto his side in time to see the horse reach the little girl, to see the lips curl back from the broad, flat teeth, to see it raise one hoof and hold it over the child's skull. He stared in shocked horror, certain he was about to see a bloody death. Across the mezzanine he heard Goldie scream.

Then the horse put its foot back down. It turned its head from side to side, looking at Deedee first with one eye, then the other. Finally it lowered itself to its knees. Gently and carefully, it put its head in the little girl's lap.

Andy pushed himself up with his arms, groaning as needles of pain shot through every bone and sinew. Nonetheless he got up and staggered over to Deedee. The horse was perfectly calm now. It ignored Andy to focus its attention on nuzzling the child. She stroked its mane. "Good horsie." She smiled at Andy.

"Right," said Andy. The room seemed to be spinning around him. He felt an arm on his shoulder. Lachtenslachter was standing beside him.

"Andy," the doctor said. "Tell me *exactly* how you got this brain."

CHAPTER SIX

"A rhinoceros?" said Andy. "No way."

"A Steppe Rhinoceros."

"Yes. I'm not an idiot, Doctor Lachtenslachter. I can tell the difference between a rhinoceros brain and a horse brain. This was a horse brain. You saw it yourself. You installed it. The brain we put in looked just like the brain we took out. And it was shelved with the other horse brains. MacGool never mentioned owning a rhinoceros brain. If he had one, he would have showed it to me."

They were gathered in the dining room, drinking coffee and eating muffins. It had been a long night.

Deedee had been able to put a rope on the horse. At her touch, it became quiescent. It let her lead it to the stable, where Andy had supplied it with hay, oats, and water, then left it locked up. Dawn was breaking when they returned to the castle. The brunt of the storm had passed, but gray skies still remained, and rain was still falling in a steady drizzle. He dried Deedee off, then sought out Doctor Lachtenslachter. He was in his laboratory, picking books out of the splintered glass and fallen shelves. He gave Andy a stack of them to bring to the dining room. He then tucked an ancient manuscript under his arm and followed Andy out.

"The Assyrians called it the Rimu," he said, after explaining to Andy that he must have taken the wrong brain. "It was noted as a wild, untamable animal of great strength and agility. The Chinese have a similar animal that they call the Zhi. But the earliest description—ah, here it is—is by Ctessis, in the Indica. He held the volume up for the others to see. The leather binding was laced with tiny cracks, and the yellow paper tore slightly when he opened it again to the page he had been studying. "'Wild white horses'," he read aloud, "'having on the forehead a horn of a cubit and a half in length, colored white, red, and black, and fleet of foot'." He put down the book and picked up another. It was also written in Latin, but it had been rebound just before Lachtenslachter bought it, so the leather still looked pretty new. "This is Pliny's Natural History. He speaks of the same animal. 'A very ferocious beast, similar in the rest of its body to the horse, with a single black horn, two cubits in length, standing out on its forehead. The legs are like a horse's and are meant for galloping'." Finally Lachtenslachter pointed to a copy of the De Natura Animalium. "Aelian says the Persians speak of a similar animal. They call it the Karadan, which translates as monoceros."

"Okay then, not an African rhinoceros. I agree that maybe it's possible that I got the brain of some kind of wild animal that looks like a horse," said Andy, "but I still think it's pretty unlikely. Maybe Finishline is right and the horse is just loco. Horses get that way. Sometimes just seeing a snake will drive them crazy for weeks. Or perhaps the shock of the transplant—Doctor Lachtenslachter, why do you think that the brain we put into the Roan Ranger came from a zhi or a rimu or a karadan?"

"A description in the Phisiologus," replied the Doctor. He reached forward to pick up yet another book, where he had marked a page with a feather quill. "Saint Ambrose, Saint Jerome, and especially Saint Basil all agree on this." He ran a finger down the page, and read, "'... it can be trapped by a virgin, for as soon as it sees her it lays its head in her lap ...'"

"Um, okay," said Andy, "But that could be just a coincidence."

"Wait a minute," said Finishline. "If you are saying what I think you are saying, then my credulity is being stretched like India rubber. Are you saying our prize-winning racehorse has been implanted with the brain of a *unicorn*?"

Lachtenslachter looked pained. "Unicorn is hardly a scientific term."

"I am not a scientific guy, Doctor. A ferocious horse with a single horn that can only be tamed by a virginal doll—that sounds like a unicorn to me." He looked at Andy, and although his voice was absolutely calm, Andy could see the question in his eyes.

Goldie voiced it. "Andy, could you have picked up the wrong brain?"

"Andy, what was the label on the jar?"

"It wasn't unicorn, Doctor Lachtenslachter, and it wasn't rhinoceros. All the labels were in different languages. Some of them were in something that looked like Hebrew, but it wasn't Hebrew."

"Chaldean. It predates the Aramaic languages."

"But this label was in Latin, and I know the first word was Elastic."

"Or something close. The beast in question is Elasmotherium sibiricum, the Steppe Rhinoceros."

Andy was silent while he digested this. After a while he said, "Oh."

Goldie stood up to stretch. She leaned over the table and picked up one of the books. It was an account of the travels of Ibn Fadlans, a volume that Lachtenslachter had consulted earlier, then set aside. A strip of green ribbon marked his page. "'There is nearby a wide steppe, and there dwells, it is told, an animal smaller than a camel, but taller than a bull. In the middle of its head it has a horn, thick and round, and as the horn goes higher, it narrows to a point like a spearhead. They are very ugly brutes to look at, but not at all such as we describe them when we relate that they let themselves be captured by virgins, but clean contrary to our notions'." She read the passage out loud.

"Thank you, Goldie," said Finishline. "Well, I think we all understand the problem now. The question is what are we going to do about it."

"Try again with the right brain," said Andy. "Maybe MacGool hasn't noticed the switch yet. If he hasn't, I can go back tonight and change this brain for the brain we want."

Finishline considered this. "That is nice of you to offer, Andy, but maybe your Doctor MacGool did notice and is lying in wait for you with a couple of constables. Never return to the scene of the crime."

"That doesn't matter," said Lachtenslachter. "Changing your brain is a bit more difficult than changing your mind. You remember that it required several days of prep work before I could install this brain. The animal needs time to recover from this operation, then I will have to sedate it, remove the existing brain and prep it again. It wouldn't recover in time for the Durk's Classic."

"We will have to take the chance," said Finishline. He looked at Goldie for confirmation. "What choice do we have? As I see it, our only other option is get a virgin to ride the horse."

He looked at Deedee, who had curled up in her chair and fallen asleep. Crumbs of muffin stuck to her nightdress.

Andy said, "I don't think so. She's much too young."

"No, I am not thinking that a small child will make a good jockey," said Finishline. "I am only looking at her because she is across the table from me and just happens to be in my line of sight."

He switched his gaze to the window, but continued to look thoughtful. Lachtenslachter and Andy both looked at Goldie. Neither man honestly thought she met the qualifications, but they were both wondering if it was ungentlemanly to show they were making that assumption. Since, however, it would also be ungentlemanly to inquire on the subject, they did not bring it up. Finishline's thoughts were moving in a totally different direction. He stirred his coffee, took a sip, and finally said, "On the other hand, there is Corduroy Brown."

Goldie said, "The girl jockey? National Cordy?"

"Who?" said Lachtenslachter.

"She is a young woman with the highest fame and regard, for last year she wins the Panjandrum National at the age of fifteen," explained Finishline. He leaned back in his chair, while he dredged the story out of his memory. "Riding her own horse, no less. She disguises herself as a boy and exchanges places with the jockey that her parents hire. She becomes an overnight celebrity, the first doll jockey in Travaillia. I am surprised that you do not hear about her."

"I don't usually read the sports page."

"The Jockey Club is furious no little, but when they see how much publicity they are getting out of it, they make a decision to go with the flow and pretend they know about it all along and that she is registered as a jockey."

"There were no rules against girls becoming jockeys," said Goldie.

"That is correct, because no stable ever tries to hire one before. Although the word is on the street that they are planning to let a few more dolls in next season. But so far, National Cordy is the only doll jockey around."

"But she doesn't race, Finishline. It was just a publicity stunt that she parlayed into a modeling career. Sure, she travels around a lot, and you see her at racetracks, but that's just because she's promoting Durk's beer or some such. You hardly ever see her on a horse."

"She is still racing once in a while, Goldie. In fact, she is entered for the Weldun Stakes tomorrow."

"Hmm, you're right. It figures that she would be in the Weldun Stakes, because that's another race that's sponsored by Durk's. But if she's racing for Durk's, then we can't hire her for the Durk's Classic. She'll already be committed."

"We will have to make a deal with the stable to release her to us. That will cost us, because she is a celebrity jockey."

"But is she qualified?" asked Lachtenslachter. "I mean qualified in the sense of our problem?"

"Will she still be unicorn bait?" said Andy.

"Well, she was fifteen when she won the Panjandrum National. So she is only sixteen now."

"Good," said Lachtenslachter approvingly. "Certainly a girl that young is still going to be innocent of any carnal knowledge."

Finishline looked at Goldie. Goldie cleared her throat. "Um, right," she said. "Certainly it is possible."

"It is by no means a sure thing, but I would give odds of seven to three that she could ride our horse. Anyway, the question is easily solved by bringing her to the horse. If the horse lets her on his back, then we do not have a problem. If it tries to bite her earlobes off, then we can fire up a grill and barbecue some horsemeat steaks, because that is all that this horse is going to be good for."

"But can we get her, Finishline? And more to the point, can we afford her?"

"I will defray the cost of hiring this girl as a jockey," said Lachtenslachter, "since it was due to our negligence that the wrong brain was installed."

"I don't think we can just walk up to her and hire her on the spot, Finishline," said Goldie. "A big stable would send their head trainer over to interview her and check her out, but if a pair of investors like us show up on her doorstep, she's likely to dismiss us out of hand."

"I am thinking you are correct, Goldie. There are a lot of dubious characters in the racing business ..."

"Hard to believe," said Lachtenslachter.

" ... and it is possible that she mistakes us for a couple of operators. We need to have a connection, a reference, someone who lets her know that we are all stand–up guys."

"Um," said Andy. Finishline, Goldie, and Lachtenslachter looked at him. He had the feeling he was going to regret telling them, but he also knew he had to do something to make up for his mistake. They waited for him to speak. He shrugged and said, "I went to school with her. Does that count?"

The Weldun Stakes was no longer considered an important race, having been overshadowed by the Durk's Classic, which was run the following week. The big brewery money pulled the more famous horses away from the smaller race. Still, any event at Geht Downs tended to be a festive occasion, more like a summer faire than a race. It was a sunny afternoon. Blue and green banners with the Durk's (the Official Beer of Geht Downs) logo hung from the stands. A band played in the center of the track. Vendors sold meat pies, sausages, and nuts from brightly painted carts. Strolling jugglers, mimes, and pickpockets worked the crowd, and everywhere were kirtled girls carrying tankards of beer. Big heavy tankards, usually three in each hand, which they dispensed with fixed smiles and the inner regret that they hadn't studied more and partied less back in school so they wouldn't have to do this for a living.

Andy stood with Finishline at the rail, watching the horses come thundering down the track. He had ridden in shows before, but it was his first time at a race track. The horses came past in a blur of dark muscle and colorful silk, throwing up clods of dirt as they went past. "Wow!" he said. "That was cool! Kind of like a stampede."

"They do not always come in a pack like that," said Finishline. "More often than not they are strung out. But it is very exciting when they all come past at once."

He pulled a tip sheet from inside his jacket pocket. "Now, Andy, I will admit that mine and Goldie's finances are seriously depleted right now. It is indeed fortunate that I am able to remedy this situation by a judicious investment in the fourth race." He showed the tip sheet to Andy. "As you can see, we are able to choose among seven horses. Do you see any you prefer?"

Andy looked the sheet over. "Silver Slurper," he read. "Out of Silver Slipper and Spaghetti."

"Meaning that the sire is Spaghetti and the dam is Silver Slipper. Silver Slurper has the fastest times but this is her first race of the summer. Avoid betting on horses that have not been out of the stable recently."

"Okay. How about Ship's Biscuit? He's fast and he raced recently."

"A good horse, but you note he is carrying more weight this race. Avoid betting horses that are carrying more weight than in their last race."

"Withering Heights," read Andy, continuing down the list. "Say La Vee. Topgallant."

"That is the one," said Finishline. "He is a five year old in a field of mostly three year olds. He has strong finishes in his last two races, but not enough of a trend to make him carry more weight. His track times are good. Usually that means the odds against him are not large and therefore the payout is small. However the odds on Topgallant are attractive enough to risk some potatoes because most people are betting on the other strong horses such as Silver Slurper and Ship's Biscuit. Furthermore, I happen to know that his jockey is a square shooter and a stand-up guy who will not throw a race, and that makes this race a very sound investment indeed. I consider this race to be such a sound investment that I am going to invest a ten spot on this horse, although I will only bet him to show because I am a cautious investor."

Andy knew that betting a horse to show meant Finishline would win if the horse came in first, second, or third. "Do your investments always pay off?"

"More than somewhat. Of course we do not win all the time. I can pick winners in one out of three races, but only a few horses are worth an investment. I only like to invest in a sure thing."

"Right," said Andy.

Finishline left him to place his bet. Andy hung over the rail, watching the jockeys and horses parade past on their way into the starting gate. Topgallant was number five and did not, to Andy's eyes, appear much different from the rest of the horses in the field. They were all bays or chestnuts, their riders were all small, grim men who looked like they knew what they were doing. But Andy wasn't paying much attention to this race. His mind was on Corduroy Brown, and what he was going to say to her, if he said anything to her at all. He had come to regret that he ever admitted he knew her.

Which was silly and he realized it. *It's not like I'm asking her on a date*, he reminded himself. *If it was a date, there's a good chance she would shoot me down, so of course I wouldn't ask her when other people were around to see me get shot down. If I was going to ask her at all. Which, of course, I'm not. This is different. This is strictly a business proposition.* He remembered that they had no other choices. If Lachtenslachter was right, the horse was not going to let any of the other jockeys mount him. Cordy was the only one they had a chance with.

Still, it would be nice not to have any adults around when he talked to her. Adults, even though they claimed to have been young at one time, seemed to suffer from major brain damage when it came to really important stuff, like talking to girls. They were constantly giving you advice like "Go ahead and ask her. What have you got to lose?" and "What's the worst that can happen? So what if she says no?" Apparently the concepts of dignity and self-respect evaporated away after you got past a certain age. Then adults wondered why you never listened to them.

He was jolted back to awareness by the sound of the starting bell. The horses took off in a pack and remained that way around the first turn. It wasn't until they reached the backstretch that they started to spread out.

"His jockey is holding him back, not wanting him to tire out," said a voice at his elbow. It was Finishline, who had suddenly reappeared. He elbowed his way to the rail as the horses came around the far turn. "See, now the jockey is giving him the whip hand, to spur him to the finish." In the final stretch Topgallant passed three other horses with what seemed to be remarkable ease and won by a full length. Andy thought it was pretty exciting. He wished he had placed a bet himself. Even though he knew there was a lot of luck involved, Finishline made it seem so easy. Finishline himself took the win calmly. "That is only what I expected. I will go and collect my winnings now, as I believe there is money to be made in the seventh race."

Before he could leave, however, a murmur ran through the crowd of betters. A scorekeeper climbed down from his ladder behind the tote board. A short pole stood by the board. Finishline suddenly looked grim. The scorekeeper ran a square of yellow cloth up the flag pole. The announcer said something that Andy couldn't make out. The scorekeeper stayed by the pole, looking for a signal from someone in the stands.

"What?" said Andy.

"The announcement is to hold on to our betting slips, because there is a dispute over the winner." They waited in silence, until the scorekeeper ran two more colored flags up the pole. He then returned to his ladder and removed Topgallant's number from the tote board. At which point Finishline tore up his betting slip in disgust.

"What?"

"The horse is disqualified, because the judges are of the opinion that the jockey is guilty of crowding another horse along the rail in the backstretch. And so you see," Finishline continued, as though he planned this whole thing as a lesson for Andy, "that it is very important to have a good jockey. A good jockey makes a lot of difference. Now we will seek out our doll."

Andy found Goldie sitting at the top of the grandstand. This was partly because the high vantage point allowed her to search the crowd more easily. And mostly because these rows of benches, lacking shelter or shade, were the cheapest seats in the stands. A wide–brimmed hat kept the sun off her skin. She passed Andy a bag of peanuts. He took it and sat down next to her. "He's onto us," he told Goldie nervously.

"Who?"

"Doctor MacGool." Andy pointed to the bottom of the stands, where Finishline was talking to an elderly man with a white beard and top hat. "That's him. Doctor MacGool is here at the track. He must have followed us. Now he's talking to Finishline. He suspects something is going on. Why else would he be here, talking to us?"

Goldie looked. "That's Doctor MacGool."

"That's what I just said."

"He's the track vet. The Jockey Club hired him. He's always here before a race. I thought you knew that."

"Oh. Right. I did. I was just surprised. This is the first time I've been to Geht Downs. Does Finishline know him?"

"I guess he does now." They watched as MacGool ended the conversation with Finishline, and then waited while Finishline made his way to the top of the grandstand. "Did MacGool say anything, Finishline?"

"Nothing that is of interest to us, sweetie." Finishline ate a peanut. To Andy he explained, "Track vets are always being questioned by investors, who would like some information as to the best way to manage their finances, particularly if it is information that the other betters do not have. So it is normal behavior for me to strike up a conversation with Doctor MacGool. However the position of track veterinarian is always occupied by people of the greatest integrity and highest ethical standards, so it is very unlikely they give out such information unless they are paid very large sums of money indeed."

"But he didn't accuse you of stealing his unicorn brain?"

"I did not bring up the subject and neither did he. But I suspect that even if he is aware of the theft, he does not associate it with us. So I suggest we concentrate on getting you in to see Miss Brown."

"What? I'm going to see Cordy? I thought we were all going to see her."

"You have to see her before we can see her," said Goldie. "You're going to introduce us to her."

"Um, I guess. But you two would have to be with me for me to introduce you to her."

"We'll stay on the sidelines, Andy. Just go up to her and say hello. Talk to her first and see how she feels about the idea. If she's agreeable, wave and we'll come over. This isn't a good time for us to approach her."

"Why not?"

"Andy, if we try to talk to her before the race, she'll be too busy preparing for it. She won't want to be interrupted. If we wait until after the race and she wins, she'll be surrounded by fans and handlers, so we won't be able to get close to her. If we wait until after the race and she loses, she might be in a bad mood and not want to listen to us. So no time is really a good time, but she's more likely to accept a visit from someone she knows."

"Wait a minute!" Andy slid down the bench, moving away from her. "I said I went to school with her. I didn't say I know her. I mean, of course I know her. I know her well enough to say hello to in the halls. But I don't know if she knows me."

It took Goldie a little bit of thinking to be certain she had this straight, then all she said was, "Andy, she is still more likely to talk to you than she will want to talk to us."

Andy was about to protest this when Finishline clarified it for him. "Figure it out, Andy. Seventeen year old boy. Sixteen year old girl. Do you see a connection, subtle though it may be?"

"Yeah, I see it. But I don't think that will do us any good. She was a hot babe to begin with. Then when she won the Panjandrum National, she was the toast of the school. I was just a science geek back then."

Finishline frowned. "And you are not a science geek now?"

"Hush, Finishline," Goldie told him. "You'll make him nervous."

"I, um, looked different then," said Andy. "I think this is a bad idea. Sorry, but it isn't going to work." He stood up. "Listen, I can pop back into MacGool's attic and get that brain tonight. I'm willing to take the risk. There's no point sticking around here, really. She won't have any idea who I am and even if she does she won't want to see me."

A young female voice interrupted him. "Andy? Is that you?"

Andy turned around. "Okay," he said. "I've been wrong

before."

A pretty girl was standing in the aisle. She was short and slim, but taut muscle betrayed a wiry strength. Her medium brown hair was covered by short-brimmed black cap. She wore a thin silver chain around her neck, and around one wrist was a silver charm bracelet with a selection of little horse head and horseshoe charms. Her medium pink lips curved up in a smile, and her medium brown eyes looked Andy over with friendly interest. She said, "What?"

"Nothing," said Andy. "Hi, Cordy."

"Wow, Andy. You look completely different."

"Um, yeah. I got my teeth fixed."

"No, there's something else about you. You look taller."

"Excuse me," said Finishline. "I think I will buy a racing form." He stepped out into the aisle and went down a few steps, stopping to wait for Goldie.

"I'll help you carry it," said Goldie.

"Yeah, I grew a bit more this year," Andy said to Cordy. "And I had a lot of dental work. I'm working with this doctor—he's got a place up in the mountains—and he was great at getting my teeth straightened. I still have to wear a retainer but ..."

Cordy stepped a bit closer. Her eyes searched his face. Her skin was fair and slightly wind burned. "No, there's something different about you now. Not just taller. I can't seem to put my finger on it, but it's there. You seem more self-assured, the way you hold yourself—I've got it! Didn't you used to be a hunchback?"

"Oh that. Yeah, Doctor Lachtenslachter also straightened my back. But it was the teeth that were the real challenge. He actually had to reshape my jaw."

"You look great."

"Thanks, so do you. But what are you doing here now? Shouldn't you be getting ready for the Weldun Stakes?"

Cordy face clouded over. "I'm not racing today. I got pulled off."

"Bummer. Why?"

"Come on, let's get something to drink and I'll tell you about it." He followed her into the clubhouse. "It will have to be Durk's," Cordy warned him. "I'm not riding their horse but I'm still under contract to them. We agreed that I can't be seen drinking anything else. On the bright side, I get it for free."

"Well, thanks. But just small beer," said Andy. "I'm not

much for drinking."

"Two small beers," Cordy told the barmaid. "I didn't know you went to the track, Andy. I've never seen you at one before."

"It's my first time here. So, aren't you still riding?"

"Huh." Cordy, Andy decided, had pretty lips even when she was frowning. "Andy, have you ever heard of a man named Waxroth?"

"Waxroth? Waxroth?" Andy looked as if he was searching his memory. "Why yes, the name sounds familiar. Kind of a bookmaker, right?"

"He's a gambler. A big one. A crooked one. He fixes everything. Horse racing, dog racing, fights, contests, pageants, elections, you name it. Everything except the tides and I wouldn't be surprised if he figured out how to fix those one of these days. Well, I don't play his game. Not even in school. Even for homecoming I wouldn't go along with it ..."

"Wait a minute," interrupted Andy. "You're saying Werner Waxroth fixed our high school beauty contest?"

"Of course. How do you think Muffy Dellwanger got elected homecoming queen?"

"I thought she was pretty."

Cordy gave Andy a sour look. "Sort of pretty," he amended hastily. "Although not in a good way."

"Uh, huh. Anyhow, I was approached a couple of times to throw a race. Not by Waxroth himself, of course. He doesn't do his own dirty work. He stays in the background and lets other people arrange things for him, so he can pretend to be an honest financier. I wouldn't go along with the program, so he decided to teach me a lesson. He leaned on the stable to pull me off the race."

"How do you know it was him?"

"The trainer didn't tell me, of course, but I found out Waxroth was behind it. Guys talk, and you hear things." Cordy took a sip from her glass. "I guess I should have expected he would do something."

Awesome, thought Andy. If he could do Cordy a favor by getting her a racing gig, that was bound to raise him a notch or two above other guys who flocked around her. "But if there are so many crooked races, why do people still bet on them?"

"That's the way gamblers are. They have to have action, and if there is no good action around, they'll take what they can get. Oh, and let me tell you, don't let gamblers rope you into any of their schemes. Like those two people you were talking to up on the grandstand? They looked like racetrack types."

"They're friends of mine," said Andy.

"If they want you to bet money with them, or for them, stay away. Don't let them talk you into it."

"Right," said Andy. "I'll remember that. But my friends aren't gamblers. I'd like to introduce them to you. They actually own a racehorse. In fact, we came here to try to see you."

It took a little persuasion. Cordy's first reaction was to put down her glass and lean back with a skeptical look. Andy thought she was going to walk out. But he talked fast, and eventually she became interested. In fact, she leaned closer as he spoke, which was not something Andy had a problem with. He didn't think he was the kind of guy to get distracted by girls, but several times when she smiled at him, he lost the focus of his narrative. Ultimately he got the whole story out, although he dispensed with the part about the unicorn brain. He merely told her they were looking for a jockey. Not that he intended to deceive her, he told himself, but it made the story just too weird, and he didn't want her to think he was a nut case. If she agreed to ride for them, he would tell her when they got back to the castle.

Cordy listened intently until he finished. She said, "So, those two gamblers you were sitting with, they're now the owners?"

"Right. Do you know them?"

"I've seen them around the tracks. Are you sure you can trust them?"

"You think they might try to stiff you on your fee? Don't worry about that. Doctor Lachtenslachter will cover that."

"I meant that Waxroth is going to fix that race. He might buy them off."

"It doesn't matter to Doctor Lachtenslachter. He just wants to see the horse run. We're not betting any money on this."

"It will be an interesting race. They ought to get great odds."

"You think so? This is a champion racehorse. Won't people see him as the favorite?"

"Not if he had a broken leg. People won't believe a horse that broke a leg will race again. They're always put down."

"I think it's cruel, myself. Why do they do that? Surely those horses can be used for general riding, or carriage horses, or something after the fracture heals."

Cordy shook her head. "It won't heal. A horse needs to stand on four legs for the blood to circulate. If they break a leg they'll die a slow, painful death. That's why it's more humane to put them down."

"What a cheerful sport racing is. I'm learning all sorts of things today."

"Oh, it's wonderful." Cordy suddenly flashed Andy a broad smile. "When I'm galloping a horse, it's like nothing else in the world. It's like the horse and I are one animal, like his muscles are my muscles. I feel like I can do anything, go anywhere, and no one can stop me. Don't you feel it?"

Andy had galloped a horse plenty of times, before his operation, and thought it felt like galloping a horse. He said, "Sure. So you're with us?"

"Let me talk to the owners."

Andy looked around and was not surprised to find Finishline and Goldie sitting two tables away, pretending to study the menu. He waved them over and made introductions. Cordy waited until they sat down before speaking. "I'll ride your horse under one condition. I'll ride a real race. No tricks, no excuses. I'm riding to win. If Waxroth tells you to hold the horse back, you'll have to find another jockey."

"There is no question of that. The word around the track is that you are not bribable. Anyway, we are not likely to find a jockey with your qualifications."

Cordy tossed her head. "Well, I did win the Panjandrum National. And I've won my share of races since then. But I have to be fair about this. There are plenty of other good jockeys available."

"When I say qualified I mean ..." Finishline stopped in mid-sentence and looked at Andy. Andy had given him a small shake of his head. They both looked at Goldie for help.

Goldie said, "What he meant, Cordy, is that we need to take you up to the castle and see if the horse likes you. He's a little temperamental. Truthfully, he's a lot temperamental. Not just anyone can ride him."

"Don't worry about it. A lot of racehorses are high-strung. I can handle them. I'm good with skittish horses. But I'm doing this because I want to give Werner Waxroth a shot in the eye. It's been one too many times that he's kept me from riding. So you'll have to find another girl if he makes a deal with you."

"Werner Waxroth," said Finishline. "Is not going to make deal with us. We have issues with Werner Waxroth."

CHAPTER SEVEN

Werner Waxroth was a big man. He wasn't tall, and he wasn't fat, exactly. He was beefy—fat with a lot of muscle in it. He had tiny eyes set in a square face and thin lips set in a straight line. His head sat on a thick neck, that connected to heavy shoulders that held arms with thick wrists. It was the kind of body that required an expensive custom shirt to look good, which was exactly what Waxroth was wearing. He looked like the kind of guy you didn't want to mess with, and in fact, no one had messed with Werner Waxroth for a very long time.

Still, he could be smooth when he wanted to be and this day he wanted to be very smooth indeed, for he was having lunch with the track veterinarian, a man named MacGool. It was part of the vet's responsibility to test the horses to make sure they were running an honest race. MacGool was, in a sense, Waxroth's adversary. Periodically Waxroth had lunch with him because Waxroth liked to keep an eye on his adversaries. MacGool was not a man who let his decisions be influenced by threats of violence. Or even by actual violence. Waxroth found this to be a regrettable lapse of judgment. He sometimes considered having MacGool bumped off in the hopes that he would be replaced with someone more pliant, but he always dismissed the idea in the end. MacGool was, after all, a type of doctor, and doctors tend to support each other. Waxroth did not care to anger the medical profession. People in his line of work called on it too often.

MacGool was having lunch with Waxroth because the veterinary business is, after all, a business, and good businessmen always try to maintain connections with others in the community. Circumstances change and MacGool might not stay the track vet forever.

But today MacGool was in a bad mood. They were in a restaurant called the Sotto Voce. It was Farlong's best restaurant. The china was thin, the wine glasses were crystal, and the silverware was plated with real silver. He had an excellent chop in front of him, and fresh spring peas, and early summer strawberries, and none of it cheered him up one whit. Even the presence of Waxroth's companion, a lovely girl with luscious pink lips and a great mass of soft red hair, failed to distract him from his problem. "They came in through the service hatch on the roof," he told Waxroth. "And went straight for the unicorn brain."

"I thought unicorns were extinct."

"Almost. That's why this one was so expensive. It will be difficult to replace. It might have been the last unicorn. In that case it will be impossible to replace. And for what? What would anyone want with a unicorn brain?"

"You bought one."

"I'm a collector. If there was anyone else around who collected brains, I'd know about it."

"Aren't unicorn horns supposed to be an aphrodisiac?"

"Ignorant superstition."

"Maybe they were superstitious."

"They stole the brain, Werner, not the head. There was no horn in that jar."

"People do strange things. Remember when the sheep ..."

"Forget about the sheep!" said MacGool. "I don't want to hear about the sheep." He stabbed at his mutton chop. "I'm sick to the bone of sheep jokes. Anyway, that's why I came to you."

Waxroth frowned. "I don't recall hearing any of my boys telling sheep jokes. But if they are, I'll certainly put a stop to it."

"Werner, I think he means he came to see you about the missing brain," said the lovely girl.

"Shut up, Diana." Waxroth gave her a look that made MacGool inwardly wince, although Diana met it with a level look of her own. "I know what he meant."

"It was the work of an organized gang," continued MacGool. "They didn't just grab any jar off the rack. They actually switched labels. They even cobbled together a duplicate brain. No, they were after the new centerpiece of my collection. They must have known what it was worth."

"You just said no one else wanted it."

"Except another collector. And there's no other collector around here. So we're dealing with an international gang, like jewel thieves. You know the kind I mean. They gather together in garrets to swill cheap gin and plot intricate crimes. Then they put on watch caps and black turtleneck sweaters and pull off fabulous capers, like this one."

Waxroth nodded. "Doctor, when you told me that someone broke into your attic, 'fabulous caper' was exactly the phrase that came to my mind."

"Yes, I'll have another glass of wine," Diana told the waiter.

"No, she won't," said Waxroth. "Diana, go powder your nose." Diana looked at him resentfully, then stood up and went to stand at the bar, where she asked for a glass of wine, only to be gently reminded that the Sotto Voce was a respectable restaurant and ladies were not permitted at the bar. She walked out.

Waxroth ignored her departure. He continued talking to MacGool. "I'm always glad to lend my assistance to a worthy cause, Doctor, but I don't know what you want from me."

"You know your way around that crowd of people. The sleazy, underworld types. You could find out if anyone was trying to fence a stolen brain."

"Me? I'm a respectable businessman."

"You're a bookie."

"A handicapper."

"And a loan shark."

"A financier."

"And an enforcer."

"What are you getting at, Doctor? Are you asking me to lean on these people?"

"Yes. No. Yes. I mean no. No, don't lean on them. I was angry before, but I'm over it. Just, you know, negotiate with them to get my brain back at a reasonable cost."

"Of course," said Waxroth thoughtfully. "Negotiating might involve leaning on them. Sometimes a broken finger or two encourages a person to come to the table."

"I don't need to know the details of your business, Werner. Just do me a favor and look for my brain." MacGool stood up and reached for his money pouch. Waxroth held up his hand. "I'll get this one, Doctor."

"No, you won't, Werner. You say that every time. You know my rule against accepting gratuities."

"Surely just a small lunch ..."

"Not even a lunch." MacGool put his silver on the table. "For appearance's sake, I shouldn't even be seen with you in public, except that it would look much worse if people thought I was trying to avoid being seen with you in public."

"Whatever you say, Doctor. I will make inquiries about your brain. And if I should need a favor in return ..."

"Any reasonable request."

"Thank you. As a matter of fact ..."

"As long as it does not involve doping horses or fixing races, of course."

"Naturally," said Waxroth. "That never crossed my mind."

"You know," Cordy told Andy, "I always wondered where you disappeared to during the summer."

"Really?" said Andy. He felt idiotically pleased that this great-looking girl thought of him when he wasn't there. "Mom and Dad started sending me to my great-uncle when I was a kid. They think mountain air is healthier. You know how the air gets down in the valley during the summer." They were in the back of Finishline and Goldie's cart, sitting on piles of wool blankets, gently swaying back and forth as the carthorse worked its way up the rocky mountain road to Barrenstock. A freshening breeze was whipping the newly budded tree limbs and flattening out the meadow grasses. Cordy's short hair made ripples across her head. "This year Deedee's parents decided to do the same thing. How are things back home, by the way?"

"Oh, same as every summer. The usual outbreaks of pox, malaria, and measles. And Black Plague, Green Plague, Yellow Plague, yellow fever, scarlet fever, typhoid fever, milk fever, diphtheria, pertussis, whooping cough, and the galloping scrots."

"No cholera?"

"Come to think of it, I haven't heard of any cases of cholera this year. I guess we've been lucky. So your parents think the air is healthier here? It certainly is colder." Cordy was wearing a light riding jacket. She pulled a blanket around herself. Andy helped adjust it over her shoulders.

"It's really quite nice when it's sunny. These summer snowstorms can be fierce, but the snow won't last long."

"Are you apprenticed to Doctor Lachtenslachter?"

"Oh no. Nothing official." Andy had long suspected that the real reason his parents began sending him to stay with relatives during the summer was that they were afraid the city kids would bully him about the hump on his back. Then, after a few years of repeating the "mountain air is healthier" line to each other, they had forgotten why they really started doing it. "I just sort of help when I'm here. He's a pretty good guy, incidentally. Don't let the villagers give you the wrong idea. They call him a mad scientist but ..."

"I know. 'Mad' doesn't mean mad as in angry. It means mad as in deranged."

"No, they mean mad as in angry. He and Eddie used to fight all the time. But he hardly ever loses his temper with anyone else."

"Oh, that's so sad. And so weird. Because you say he never gets mad at you?"

"I guess it's different when it's not your own kid. My parents say he concentrated too much on the scientific aspects of bringing a human to life and wasn't prepared for the responsibilities of parenthood."

"Here comes the snow," Goldie called back over her shoulder. Fat white flakes began drifting down. They looked quite pretty at first, sparkling in the setting sun. In a few minutes more the wind increased, and the flakes grew smaller and dove into the ground at a slant. Fortunately they were past the steepest part of the journey, and Finishline was able to get the horse into a trot, as he did not want to drive the wagon in a snowstorm in the dark. Goldie lit their lantern. When they turned away from Barrenstock there was still some light left in the sky, enough to see a lone figure walking the road from the village to the castle, bundled up in a parka and leaning into the wind.

"Is that him?" said Cordy.

"That's him," confirmed Andy. "He had a few errands in the village this morning." Finishline brought the cart to a halt. "Doctor Lachtenslachter, hop in." Andy put out his hands for the Doctor to grab, then pulled him up into the wagon. Finishline urged the horse into motion again. Andy did the introductions. "Doctor Lachtenslachter, this is Corduroy Brown."

"Delighted, Miss Brown." Lachtenslachter took her hand gravely. "Horse racing is a dangerous profession, I understand, with a high risk of slips, falls, and throws. Have you been injured recently?"

"Not at all," said Cordy cheerfully.

Lachtenslachter looked disappointed. "Well, let me know if it ever happens. Modern technology has given us medical techniques that are far superior to mere healing."

Cordy looked puzzled at this, but Lachtenslachter turned the conversation to other subjects. He asked her a series of polite but probing questions, mostly about her riding experience, until they reached the castle. "Have you eaten, Miss Brown? How about you, Andy? We can go back to the inn if anyone is hungry."

"I'm good," said Andy.

"So am I," said Cordy. "Goldie and I had small beer and fried pies at the racetrack."

Mrs. Barley opened the door before the cart stopped

moving. "Ah, there you are, Doctor Lachtenslachter." She wore her coat over her house dress and had a lantern already in hand. "The sky does not look good, Doctor Lachtenslachter, so I sent the servants home early. I put Deedee to bed. She already had her supper. I left a potted chicken on the stove for you, and there is a fresh loaf in the bread box. Be sure they eat something," she said to Goldie. "You know how men are. They won't take care of themselves. Left to their own devices, they'd live on nothing but beer and fried pies."

"They're helpless without us," Goldie agreed.

Lachtenslachter had climbed out of the wagon by the time Mrs. Barley finished. He took her hands. "My dear woman, where are you going? You can't possibly walk back to Barrenstock. I insist you spend the night."

"Pshaw," said Mrs. Barley, which surprised Cordy. She didn't think anyone actually said, "Pshaw", even in the country. "Don't worry about me, Doctor. Why, I've been walking up and down these roads, winter and summer, since I was a little girl. A fresh summer snow doesn't worry me. It just makes it easier to see."

Lachtenslachter insisted again while he paid her for watching Deedee, but Mrs. Barley was equally insistent that she had work to do at the inn, and a short time later was marching down the village road. Andy reflected that she was probably right. It was easier to see. The moon was rising behind the castle, obscured by only a thin layer of snow clouds that made the whole sky seem brighter.

But the night air was cold, and the wind was cutting, and he was glad to get inside and shed his coat with the others. Everyone was tired, but Cordy wanted to see the horse. She and Goldie went upstairs to change clothes. Andy brought up Cordy's carpetbag, then returned downstairs to do his back exercises.

Twenty minutes of exercise got his blood pumping and the chill out of his bones. He had almost completed his routine when he heard a giggle. He turned around to find Cordy watching him. "Sorry," she said. "I didn't mean to interrupt. But what are you doing? Are you shadow–boxing?"

"Exercising," Andy told her. "It's called *Noh Kandu*. It's an ancient exercise system from the far east."

"It looks like you're fighting in slow motion."

"You're not too far wrong. *Noh Kandu* is both an exercise system and a martial art. When you do the movements slowly, it tones the body, focuses the mind, relaxes the nerves, and improves the circulation. It also prevents the common cold."

"But does it cure acne?"

"Well, it reduces it. Also it eliminates athletes' foot, cures dandruff, and restores your hair's natural shine and body. And if you do the exercises quickly and forcefully, you have a complete system of self–defense. Doctor Lachtenslachter hired an Asian martial arts guru to teach it to me."

"What are you focusing your mind on now?"

"This movement is called 'Climb Mountain, Return to Ocean'. The idea is that you have completed the last movement and are preparing for the next wave of motion." Andy did complicated circular things with his hands and feet. "Then this movement translates as 'Bite the Wax Tadpole'. Except I have a sneaking suspicion that the words in our language fail to convey the true meaning."

Goldie came down the stairs wearing her fox coat. "Are you two ready? Let's get Finishline and Doctor Lachtenslachter and see the horse."

They went out to the stables together. Lachtenslachter led the way, cheerfully telling Cordy about his numerous medical breakthroughs, in particular his ingenious methods for restoring severed nerves, reversing the effects of gangrene, curing heart disease, and updating old tattoos to cooler, trendier designs. Finishline and Goldie trailed behind Cordy, nervously waiting to see how the horse would react to her presence. Andy walked beside her, carrying a spill proof patent lantern to use in the stables.

Inside, the stable was dark and silent, which Andy decided was a good sign, since he figured it meant the horse was either asleep or feeling particularly calm. He stood aside while the rest of the group filed in after him, then shut and latched the stable door, so the horse couldn't escape if it went on a rampage. The lantern was hooked onto a chain that hung from the ceiling. It was meant to keep flame away from the walls, which were more likely to catch fire, but it left the Roan Ranger's stall in deep shadow, and Andy couldn't quite see inside. But Andy was quite certain he was still there, because he and Deedee had fed the him and left him there that morning, and there was no way the hired stable hand was going to move this horse. He took precautions against the chance that the horse might freak out again. He positioned Cordy in front of the stall, but well back from the door, so she could see inside but be out of harm's way if the horse got crazy. He made a lasso in the end of a coil of rope, and slung it over his shoulder. Cordy watched this with patience and a bit of amusement. Finishline, Goldie, and Lachtenslachter, who knew what Andy was doing, watched without comment. When everyone was in position and waiting expectantly, Andy flung open the stall door, exposing its occupant to Cordy's eager eyes.

Except there was no occupant. The horse was gone.

"What the hell?" said Finishline, and Andy couldn't have put it better himself. He quickly opened the doors to the stalls on either side of the horse, just in case his memory was playing tricks on him. They too were empty. The stable held six stalls. Andy opened all of them. Deedee's pony tried to nuzzle his sleeve. Finishline's dray horse looked at him quizzically.

"He's gone," Andy said, stating the obvious.

Goldie looked as if she were about to cry. "Our horse is gone!"

"There's no need to panic," said Lachtenslachter. "He simply got loose and wandered off. He's probably not far away."

"His stall was closed," Andy pointed out. "And the stable door was latched. He didn't get out by himself."

"Andy is correct." Finishline's eyes were narrow, his voice stern. "I am thinking that some miscreant is in possession of our racehorse."

"MacGool?" said Goldie, although doubtfully. "He came to take his brain back?"

"Any strangers passing through would immediately be noticed in a small village like Barrenstock," said Andy. "Especially if they took the road to the castle. Doctor Lachtenslachter was there all day. Someone would have told him."

"Quite right," said Lachtenslachter. "The simplest explanation is that one of the cleaning women or the stable hand rode him back to town. It is a blustery night and someone decided not to walk home."

"Not one of your maids," said Goldie. "I've talked to everyone who works here. Not one of them can ride that horse."

"Why not?" said Cordy, who didn't comprehend any of this. "Why couldn't someone else ride your horse?"

No one had a chance to answer, as Andy heard a slight sniffle coming from the end of the stable. He took the lantern back to the last stall. Deedee's pony whickered. He pushed it aside and held the lantern forward, so he could see into the corner. A spot of pink caught his eye. "Oh, for goodness sake." He reached under the straw, grabbed Deedee's shoulder, and yanked the little girl to her feet. "Deedee, what are you doing here?"

"Nothing," said Deedee sullenly.

"Never mind nothing. What happened to the racehorse?"

Deedee stuck her lip out. "I don't know."

The others gathered around Andy. Deedee stood in a halo of light from the stable lantern. Straw stuck out of her hair and clung to her pink flannel nightdress.

"Her feet are bare," said Goldie. "Deedee, you'll catch your death of cold."

"Deedee, you should be in bed," said Lachtenslachter. "I'll carry you back up to the house."

He moved forward, but Finishline put an arm out to stop him. "Just a minute, Doctor." He looked at Deedee sternly. "Okay, little doll. Tell me who is absconding with our thoroughbred?"

"What?"

"Where is the horse?"

"I don't know."

"Little doll, I am very much interested in knowing what happened to our racehorse."

Deedee clung to her pony's neck. "I don't know. I just came here to be with Patches."

"Don't badger the child, Finishline," said Goldie.

"Hang on," said Andy. "Let me talk to her." He knelt down next to the girl and put an arm around her little shoulders. "Deedee," he said gently. "I know your parents don't believe in spanking children, right?"

Deedee looked at him uncertainly. "Right."

"And we know that my parents feel the same way. So does Doctor Lachtenslachter. They believe that spanking is ineffective and teaches a little girl the wrong message. They think that violence against children is never justified, and that gentle methods of discipline will encourage better behavior. Isn't that right?"

Deedee nodded enthusiastically. "Yes! Spanking is bad!"

"Well, Deedee, there is something you need to remember. I'm not your mother or your father or your uncle. I'm your cousin, and if you don't tell me where that horse is right this minute I'm going to *wallop your bottom so hard you won't sit for a week!*"

"It's his fault," shouted Deedee right back. She pointed to Finishline. "He was going to kill the horsie. I told it to run away."

"What is she talking about? I am not going to kill the horsie—I mean—our racehorse."

"I heard you," said Deedee accusingly. "You were talking to Mickey." Mickey was the stable hand. "You said if the horsie won, you would send him to Paradise. We learned about Paradise in Sunday school. It's where good people go when they die."

"For goodness sakes, kid. I am not in the habit of killing horses, particularly if they are winning horses, which is a custom that I strongly believe should be encouraged in horse society. When I say that I am sending a horse to Paradise, I mean that I am considering sending him to a stud farm."

Deedee looked at Finishline suspiciously. "What's a stud farm?"

"It is a place to where all men aspire to go. But only the very best animals get sent there."

"Shush, Finishline." Goldie knelt next to Deedee. "Deedee, a stud farm is a very nice place, a place where the Roan Ranger would ... would ... make new friends. Lots and lots of new friends. He would be very happy there. But we are not sending him to a stud farm anyway. We're going to keep him with us."

"Yes," added Cordy helpfully. "We'll take him to racetracks, where he can do the thing that stallions love to do best."

All the men looked at her.

"I mean run," she explained. "Racehorses love to race. It's in their blood."

"Right," said Andy. "That's what I thought you meant. So Deedee, where is the Roan Ranger?"

Deedee began to cry. "I let him go. I thought you were going to kill him. I told him to run away and he did."

Finishline was at the stable door in a flash. Andy was right behind him, holding him back. "There's no point running out in the darkness." He closed the door against the cold wind and the swirl of dry snow. "You don't know these mountains. You'll just get lost yourself. We're better off if we take a few minutes and work up a plan."

"Andy is right," said Lachtenslachter. "The first thing to do is return to the house and get warm clothing and more lanterns. Deedee, which way did the horse go?"

Deedee stopped sniffling long enough to go to the door and point into the darkness. Andy picked her up and exchanged a glance with Doctor Lachtenslachter. "The ravine." They started up the garden path that led to the castle.

Finishline hurried up behind them. "I am experiencing a cold feeling."

"It is cold out," said Lachtenslachter. "It's freezing, in fact. But that is not unusual in these mountains."

"This cold feeling I am having is in the pit of my stomach, which is not a place where I usually get cold feelings. However I get this cold feeling when I hear you say 'the ravine.' What is the ravine?"

"It's not that steep." Andy tried to reassure him. "Um, but a horse might have trouble getting out of it again if he stumbled into it."

"Right," said Lachtenslachter, "and he would, at least, be sheltered from the wind."

"Of course he might flounder in a snow drift. The snow tends to drift up in the ravine."

"But then a snowdrift might cushion his fall if he fell into it."

"I think I am getting the picture," said Finishline. "And it is not a pretty picture. It is a type of picture as might be painted by an artist who drinks absinthe and talks about angst."

"Not to worry," said Lachtenslachter. "This is a steppe rhinoceros, don't forget. It was raised in conditions that are far more severe than anything we get in Travaillia. It is quite accustomed to cold weather and inhospitable terrain."

"It has the brain of a unicorn, Doctor. It has the body of a thoroughbred racehorse and it is quite accustomed to a warm stable and a level racetrack." Andy and Lachtenslachter could make no reply.

Cordy walked alongside Goldie. "Why do you call this horse the Roan Ranger? The papers list it as a bay."

"We didn't name it. Anyway, it doesn't matter. This isn't the type of horse that comes when you call it."

"That's good. Because if I'm going to freeze to death running out into a storm calling my beloved horse's name ..."

"I read the same kind of book when I was your age," said Goldie.

" ... I don't want it to be the Roan Ranger."

They caught up with the rest of the group as they reached the side door to the castle. Andy led the way to the cloak room, then went to collect lanterns while the rest of the party donned overcoats, scarves, and galoshes, except for Goldie, who had stylish boots with heels. When he came back Lachtenslachter was giving instructions.

"The slope to the north of the stable, where Deedee said the horse went, is divided by a steep ravine," he explained. "We'll split into three groups. Since we know the area, Andy will take one side of the ravine and I'll take the other. If we find the horse, we'll drive it back this way. The rest of you can wait by the stable."

Cordy looked at Lachtenslachter and clearly decided he was too old to go out in a mountain snowstorm alone. "We don't all need to wait at the stable. I'll go with you."

"All right, Miss Brown. Follow me." Andy waited until they were out of earshot, then said, "What we need is one girl on each team to attract the horse. Deedee, do you want to ride your pony?"

"Yes!" Deedee nodded her head so hard her little body bounced.

Andy hustled to get a blanket and saddle on Patches. "I'm going to lead you. Stay on the pony and tell me if you get too cold."

"I will go with you," said Finishline, who was not about to wait at the stable while his life savings were roaming around in a storm. "You cannot watch after the little doll and search for the horse at the same time."

"I'll go too," said Goldie.

"Sweetie, someone needs to stay behind in case the horse returns."

"Hmm." Goldie nodded. "Yes, you're right."

"Don't try to catch it. Just open the stable door and hope he goes in by himself."

And thus equipped with freshly filled storm lanterns and heavily armed with lumps of sugar, the brave trio turned into the night, their feet making muffled clumps against the thin layer of snow. Except for Deedee, who was bundled up in layers of clothing that left her nearly unable to move. Andy set her on her pony and guided her feet in the tiny stirrups. Despite her initial excitement, the child slumped forward and quickly dozed off. "Do you think he will recognize the little doll?" asked Finishline. He had to raise his voice to be heard against the wind. "Right now she has the shape of a potato."

"I don't think unicorns go by looks. I think they have a sixth sense about these things. He'll be attracted to either Deedee or Cordy."

"Let us hope his sixth sense works through snow. I think they must be like mosquitoes."

"Mosquitoes aren't attracted only to girls."

"No, but they are attracted to some people more than others. And somehow they know when people are around and come swarming out of the shadows."

A particularly fierce gust of wind blew a clump of snow off a pine branch. It spattered on Andy's head. He wiped his face with a gloved hand. "I'm hoping that this horse is attracted to a memory of a nice, warm stable and a bin full of oats." Andy had confidence. He was familiar with the mountain after having spent many summers here. He had heard many ballads, and read many stories, about people who had gone out in cold stormy nights to find a lost child, dog, horse, boyfriend, girlfriend, or an in–law who owed them money. And eventually they did find them. The lost soul would be lying on a snow bank, lips blue with cold, and sometimes might have to lose a few toes to frostbite, but they were always rescued in the end. The searchers never came home, shrugged off their jackets, and said, "Nope, couldn't find 'em. Got any cocoa?"

Finishline, on the other hand, had little experience with the great outdoors. He was not an athletic person. For him, fresh air and exercise were best obtained by opening a window. Crossing rough terrain on a cold, snowy night struck him as the sort of thing only done by intrepid explorers who later had rivers named after them. His lantern provided enough light to see Andy, Deedee, the pony, and driving grains of snow. Beyond that white powder, he was sure, lurked monsters whose chief desire was to chow down on a prize–winning thoroughbred and who no doubt studied the Racing Form to select their evening snack.

He shivered. "I am myself finding the idea of a hot bowl of oats and a warm bed of hay attractive," he told Andy. "Is there anything in these woods that will attack a horse?"

"Sure. Puma, bears and wolves ..."

"Um."

"... but they're probably all snug in their dens on a night like this. They won't be out hunting."

"Yes, that is most likely."

"Unless they're really hungry. The big danger is that he might fall ..."

And at that point Finishline's foot went through a hole in the snow. His body followed it, slipping through the thin, frozen crust into empty air. He flung out his arms, sending his lantern flying. Something solid touched his wrist. Instantly he grabbed onto it. It turned out to be Andy's hand.

"... into the ravine. Hold on." Finishline was dangling over the edge of a precipice. Andy was holding him up for now, but Andy's footing was not stable either. He slipped along the treacherous ground. Luckily he was holding the pony's reins in his other hand. Four hooved feet dug into the ground and gave them the extra traction they needed. Andy cautiously coaxed the pony to take a few steps forward until he could transfer the reins to Finishline. Finishline let go of Andy and grabbed the reins with both hands. Andy grabbed a handful of mane and urged the pony backward until it had pulled them all to safe ground. Deedee slept through it all.

"Don't walk so close," Andy told Finishline, giving advice that was, at this point, totally unnecessary. "It's slippery on the edge." He held his own lantern above his head and peered down. Finishline realized for the first time they had been walking along the brink of a steep slope. A few yards away he could see that the tops of trees were even with his head. Their trunks rose from the bottom of the ravine. He looked down, to where his own lantern, still burning, cast a small circle of light below. "I am not seeing anything. Is there anything that you are seeing?"

"No," said Andy cheerfully. "Which is good. It means he didn't fall into it. If we saw him down there, that would be bad. Look over there."

Finishline looked and saw two halos of light glowing yellow in the pale moonlight.

"Cordy and Doctor Lachtenslachter" said Andy. "We're coming to the end of the ravine. Then we can cross behind it and meet them. Come on."

It took another hour to reach the end of the ravine and move down the slope, where Cordy and Lachtenslachter were waiting for them. By that time the snow had stopped falling. The wind had dropped off and the sky had partly cleared. On the downside, it had gotten colder. Cordy was clapping her hands together for warmth. "Did you see anything on your side?" Andy asked them both.

Cordy shook her head. "No, but it's very dark down there, and there's trees and bushes. I suppose we might have missed him."

"We wouldn't have missed him. A bay horse on a white background? I think he would be easy to see."

"Not if he was dead and covered with snow."

"He wouldn't be dead." Lachtenslachter was certain about this. "A fall like that won't kill either a horse or a man. It would just cripple him. We'd see movement and he would probably make a lot of noise. It is far more likely that he went off in another direction."

Although this was meant to be reassuring, Finishline did not find it so. "Then what is he doing now? Is he going into the woods, with the lions and bears and wolves?"

"Possibly," said Cordy. "In weather like this his instinct will be to shelter under a tree."

"Or return to the stable," said Finishline hopefully.

"Quiet everyone," Andy said. He was looking at the tree line. "I think I saw something." He held his lantern up, so it cast its light farther, and so the flame wouldn't be directly in his line of sight and ruin his night vision.

It got ruined anyway, because Cordy and Lachtenslachter immediately ran to his side and held their lanterns in front of them. Everyone looked where Andy was looking. The snow encrusted pines formed a picket line of black trunks, white crowns, and charcoal gray space in between. Finishline, who no longer had a lantern, was the first one to speak. "Yes! Over there. I see something move."

Lachtenslachter peered into the darkness. "A swirl of snow, perhaps."

"No, it is not white. It is like a shadow."

"Was it the size of a horse?"

"I cannot tell you. It is not really a horse that I am seeing. It is just a shadow of movement."

Andy came to a decision. "Let's fan out and move in that direction. If one of us sees the horse, try to surround it." He thought about what he said. "That didn't come out right. I mean if one of us sees the horse, point it out and we'll all try to surround it."

"Or better still," said Lachtenslachter, "get on the far side of it so we can herd it back to the stable."

"That is a sensible plan," said Finishline, "except that it does not take into account the aforementioned lions, bears, and wolves, of which previously we are having some discussion."

"You don't have a lantern anyway, so you need to stay with Deedee. Cordy, spread out over that way. Doctor Lachtenslachter can take the middle, and I'll move over here—yow!"

The horse appeared out of the darkness with a speed and suddenness that would have made a striking cobra whip out a notepad and ask for training tips. The searchers should not have been startled. They were looking for a racehorse, after all, and they all knew racehorses ran fast and were quick out of the starting gate, and they all hoped that this one was not only true to type but an exceptional example of it. So they should have been prepared, but they were not. Cordy gave a little screech. Lachtenslachter dropped his lantern. Finishline uttered a short, descriptive phase popular among stable hands. Andy took a step backwards, lost his balance, and sat down in the snow. Even Deedee's pony gave his harness bells a shake. Deedee woke up, looked around and murmured, "Horsie?"

The Roan Ranger ran straight at Andy. He couldn't do anything but stare. It loomed over him, rearing back on its hind legs, metal-sheathed hooves sawing the air, a huge dark monster framed by a moonlit sky. Light from the lanterns reflected in its eyes, filling them with orange flame, like a creature that had escaped from Hell and was bringing souvenirs home inside its skull. It let out an angry bellow and in the sound Andy could hear the anger of a wild creature, an untamed creature, one that roamed the steppes and fought with any living thing that came into sight. It came down hard on all four feet, one of the front hooves hitting a patch of bare rocks and striking sparks, the other front hoof slamming onto the ground just inches away from Andy's thigh. It turned its head to the side and one eye focused on him with savage intensity. Paralyzed with shock, Andy couldn't move. Dimly he could hear the others shouting. He said nothing, but continued to stare into the horse's eyes while he scrambled backward. Only a few feet of this, however, brought him to the edge of the ravine. He realized he could not escape. The horse stalked him, moving forward as Andy moved backward, its hooves making a hard, crunching sound in the dry snow. Andy knew this was the end, that the horse would not be satisfied until Andy was trampled to death. It was a wild animal trapped in the body of a domestic horse and it was not happy. He steeled himself for the first blow.

And then the horse carefully knelt in the snow and rested its head on Andy's lap.

Cordy was the first one to break the silence. She said, "Okay everyone, is there something about this horse you haven't told me?"

CHAPTER EIGHT

***"What the hell is this?"* said Waxroth.** He was in his office. It was an expensive office, paneled in rosewood, with custom-crafted furniture and oil paintings of landscapes and lighthouses. The carpet was closely woven and imported from Tabriz. The sideboard held a bowl of wax fruit.

The office was located over a candy store. Most candy stores attract children, but children never shopped at this candy store because the prices were five times higher than anywhere else. The jars of bulls' eyes, toffees, licorice whips, and peppermint sticks had thick coatings of dust on them. The jar of lollies hadn't been opened in ten years. All of the candy store's customers were grown men, who only passed through it on their way to the large back room, or to go up the side stairs to Waxroth's office.

The office tended to get stuffy in the summer, because it didn't have windows. Waxroth didn't want anyone to be able to look inside when he was having meetings. It had a thick, heavy, soundproof door. The door didn't have a lock, because Waxroth didn't want anyone listening at the keyhole. When Waxroth wanted privacy, one or two of his men stood in the hallway to tell visitors to stay out, and when Waxroth's thugs wanted you to stay out, you stayed out.

The office was pretty big, as offices go, but at this time it seemed small because Waxroth, who was a big man, took up nearly all the space behind the desk, and Grogan, who was a very large man indeed, took up most of the space in front of the desk. It was fortunate for Diana that she was a slender girl, for there was only a little room left for her to stand behind Waxroth and massage his shoulders. This merely irritated him, however, and he shrugged her hands away. "Get me a drink."

Diana obeyed the order silently. She went to a sideboard, uncorked a crystal decanter, and poured three tumblers of whiskey. She set one in front of Waxroth, gave one to Grogan, and kept one for herself. Waxroth, who had not meant for her to play host to Grogan, glared at her, but she simply brushed her long red hair off her shoulders and pretended not to notice.

"What is what, Boss?" said Grogan.

A broadsheet lay open on Waxroth's desk. He tapped it. "It says here that the Roan Ranger is running in the Durk's Classic. It's a mistake. The Roan Ranger is dead. They can't have a second horse with the same name. It screws up the stud books. They should have scratched his name from the starting list by now."

"Nah, Boss. It's the same horse. They didn't put it down."

"They had to put it down. It had a broken leg. I saw it."

"I guess they decided to fix it."

"You can't fix a broken leg on a racehorse."

"I guess that's why the odds on it are so good. I went and looked it over myself. The leg looks just fine."

"The leg might look fine but the bones haven't knitted. That takes months. The owners must be crazy. Who the hell would ..." He paused a moment to scan the paper on his desk. "Finster and Theis?"

"Finishline and Goldie, Boss. Yep."

"Those two losers bought a racehorse?"

"What I think, Boss," said Grogan, settling back in his chair as much as he could settle in a normal sized chair. "What I think is that they realized they are never gonna pay off the money they owe you and they are desperate. Desperate enough to gamble on a long shot and run a racehorse with a recently healed injury. I dunno if it can run, though. I think it's in a lot of pain."

"Why do you say that?"

"It's gotten feisty. The stable hands say it used to be an even–tempered horse. Now they can't even touch it. Finishline and Goldie brought some teenager in to take care of it. For some reason it likes kids. They hired National Cordy to ride it. None of the other jockeys can get near it."

Waxroth's face did not change expression immediately. It was something Grogan had seen before, something that Waxroth did when he was playing cards or watching a sucker sign for a loan with a ruinously high interest rate. A good card player knows how to put on a poker face, to adopt a neutral expression that won't betray his emotions. But a really good card player knows how to convey the emotion he wants to show. As Grogan watched, Waxroth carefully composed his features into an expression of mild disinterest. "Really?"

"Yeah," Grogan said.

Without turning his head, Waxroth said, "Diana, go make

yourself pretty."

Diana gave him an angry look, which was wasted, since he wasn't looking at her. She drained her glass and left. Waxroth waited until she closed the door. "I find it suspicious that a horse with a broken leg is ready to run again. Find out what vet they used."

"They didn't use anyone around here, Boss. I hear they took it to some town up in the mountains."

"Find out the name of the town."

"Barrenstock, Boss."

Waxroth looked surprised. "You know this?"

"You told me to keep track of Finster and Theis, Boss," Grogan reminded him. "In case you wanted me to bring them in for a little chat."

"So I did. Good job, Grogan. Barrenstock, hmmm. They must have a good vet in Barrenstock?" Waxroth said this although he knew it wasn't true. He wanted to hear Grogan's response.

Grogan shook his head. "No, Boss. There's only a few vets that can perform surgery on a racehorse and they're all going to be located near racing stables. There's no racing stables in those mountains."

"Correct." Waxroth drummed the fingers of his left hand on the broadsheet. "But there was a famous surgeon who retired there a few years back."

"Dunno, Boss."

"Are they feeding it painkillers?"

"No, Boss." Grogan was sure of himself. "MacGool was all around that horse when it came back. He'd have detected any doping."

Waxroth actually laughed. It wasn't pleasant laughter. Grogan had heard the term 'sardonic laughter' once, and he guessed he was listening to it now. "What's funny, Boss?"

"MacGool. Sometime the thing we're looking for is right under our nose and we can't see it."

"What?"

"Never mind. Grogan, I don't want that horse to run. I've invested a lot of money in this race and I don't want any wild cards showing up and changing the odds. Broken leg or no broken leg."

Grogan brightened. "You want me to lean on Finishline, Boss? I could do that. I wouldn't mind doing that at all."

"No, I don't want you breaking Finster's arm."

"Are you sure? I think he has it coming to him. He's kind

of a smartass, you know. Guys like that need to be put in their place. And you know he can't pay off his marker. Goldie neither. I could break each of their arms."

"Breaking their arms isn't going to stop their horse from running. I want you to ..."

"I could break their legs. I haven't done a leg in a long time. A couple of months, at least. I don't normally do legs, you know, but this time it would be kind of poetic. The horse and the owners, all with broken legs."

"Shut up about the broken legs. Go find that new kid. Lancet is his name. Tell him I got a job for him. I want you to go with him, to watch his back."

"Go with him where, Boss?"

"To find Cordy. He is going to stop her from riding that horse."

"Now we're getting somewhere," Grogan said enthusiastically. He downed the rest of his whiskey. "You want me to show him how to break the girl's arm? I can do that. I think it's good for the younger generation to learn these things. So many kids are out there with no training. Someone just gives them an ice pick or piece of lead pipe, sends them out on the street, and expects them to do a professional job. It's a crying shame. Of course," he finished thoughtfully, "Finishline and Goldie would just get another jockey."

"No," said Waxroth firmly. "I don't think they would. Anyway, neither one of you is going to break her arm. We've been breaking too many arms lately. It's like any other method of persuasion. You use it too much, it loses its effectiveness. No, we're going to take a different approach this time. I want Lancet to violate her."

"To what?"

"To force himself on her."

"That's going to stop her from riding?"

"It will."

"I don't think so, Boss. Some girls go all to pieces after something like that. But others bounce right back. I think Cordy is the bounce back kind."

"This is a special case."

Grogan considered his boss. Waxroth had been involved in some pretty complicated schemes. They made him a lot of money, but he didn't care to explain exactly how they worked, at least not to Grogan. Waxroth had always made it clear that Grogan was an underling who was expected to follow orders. He wasn't supposed to ask questions, unless he had to ask questions to make sure he understood his orders. Grogan made sure now. "You want Lancet to make out with the girl?"

"Seduction isn't what we're talking about, Grogan. This isn't meant to be a treat for her. I want him to be rough about it. Corduroy Brown has been trouble for me. It's time she learned that in this business, you have to go along to get along."

"Boss, if that's what you want, you don't need Lancet. I can do the job myself." Grogan smiled, showing a mouthful of chipped teeth. "It won't be any trouble at all."

Waxroth's mind was already switching to other matters. He pulled an account book in front of him. Without looking up he said, "You're too ugly."

"That's because you're looking at me full on. I have a classic profile."

This time Waxroth did look up. Grogan obligingly turned his head to one side. Waxroth said, "Your profile looks like it was trampled on by a herd of camels."

"Aw."

"Grogan, you look like a big, mean, tough, thug. You're supposed to look like a big, mean, tough, thug. That's why I hired you. It makes you more effective, when I send you out to do something mean and tough, that you look the part. But if a pretty young girl like National Cordy says that a thug like you raped her, everyone is going to believe her. No one will question her word, even if I get five guys to swear that you were at a card game on the other side of town that day. It will be different when she accuses a young, handsome, stylishly-dressed kid like Lancet. When he acts all innocent and says it was consensual, a lot of people will give him the benefit of the doubt. The matter will be dropped. As an added bonus, any blot on her reputation will scuttle her contract with Durk's beer. So she'll be less inclined to refuse my next offer."

Grogan looked doubtful, but accepted this. "Okay, Boss. I'll get Lancet and tell him what to do."

Waxroth turned a page in his account book and dipped a quill in red ink. "Do that. And send Diana back in."

When Diana returned Waxroth was deep in calculations. She closed the door quietly behind her, crossed the room, and put a hand on his shoulder. He shrugged it off. Without looking up, he said, "Be dressed for dinner at seven. Wear something formal tonight. It's a dinner party. I want you to look your best. Get your hair done if you think you need it."

"All right, Werner."

"And I want you to stay sober tonight."

"Yes, Werner. Will we be going somewhere after dinner?"

"No. I will be staying afterward to play cards. You'll go home."

"I thought we could spend some time together." Diana did her best to sound suggestive, and her best was very suggestive indeed. She shifted her weight, and suddenly her curves seemed that much curvier, her lips more luscious, her hair poofier. It would take an exceptional man to ignore the invitation in her voice. "We could light a fire, and some candles, and open a bottle of ..."

"I'll be playing cards until late. Don't wait up."

Diana's attitude changed from tropical heat to midwinter chill. She gave him a look that could have frozen a snow goose in flight. It was wasted, since all he showed her was the back of his head. Finally she said, "Yes, Werner."

"It's a slut unicorn," Andy explained.

"A what?"

"I mean it! It's a totally different breed of unicorn. They're attracted to non-virgins. They wear ankle-strap horseshoes."

"Andy," said Lachtenslachter patiently, "you're seventeen years old. No one expects you to be experienced. There's no reason to be embarrassed."

"Well, yeah. I guess not. But still."

It was several days after the storm. They were all back in the City of Farlong, back at Geht Downs, where Lachtenslachter and Andy were watching Cordy exercise the Roan Ranger. They had all been up since early morning, before the racing started, when the track was open for practice. At first the Roan Ranger had balked at the bridle and bit, but before long Cordy had him trotting in brisk circles around the infield. Half a dozen other handlers had their horses on the track. They called friendly greetings to her, which she returned with a smile and a nod. The sun was out, the day was warm, and in the center of the track wildflowers were blooming in profusion. A light breeze kept the flies away. It was a perfect day for riding. Andy leaned on a fencepost and rested his chin on his arms. With a moody expression he watched Cordy exercise the horse.

"A girl who doesn't do it is considered virtuous. She's admired for it. A guy who hasn't done it is considered a loser. He doesn't want the fact pointed out to everyone who walks past."

"Andy, it will hardly be pointed out to everyone who walks past. It won't be pointed out to anyone, in fact. Outside of our little circle here, no one knows that the horse has the brain of a unicorn, and since everyone except Miss Brown participated in the switch, we're hardly likely to talk about it. Even Miss Brown has agreed to become part of our deception. The Roan Ranger appears to be an ordinary horse. The world is full of bad-tempered horses."

"Cordy goes to my school. You don't know what the other girls at my school are like. Most of them only talk about three things; clothes, make-up, and boys. But those three subjects, they talk about them to death. If they found out about— okay, I know that most guys my age have never done it. But a few have, so the rest of us have to pretend we're one of those few."

"I think you're putting too much importance on this, Andy." Cordy waved to them. They waved back. They watched as she slowed the Roan Ranger and walked it toward the fence. Lachtenslachter continued, "Even if this horse was visibly a unicorn, few people would care that it lets you handle it. No one would laugh at you."

The Roan Ranger stretched its neck over the rail and nuzzled Andy's shoulder. Cordy laughed. Andy pushed it away. He waited until she took the horse onto the track again. Then he turned to glare at Lachtenslachter. "See."

"I expect she just thought of something funny."

"Yeah, right."

"Andy, I'm certain Miss Brown can be trusted to keep your deep, dark secret. What do you think, Mrs. Theis?" Lachtenslachter said as Goldie approached. She was wearing a light suede jacket and a straw hat. "In your opinion, can women be relied upon to keep secrets?"

"Not all of them," said Goldie. She took off the hat and fluffed her hair a bit. "You would be surprised. A couple of times Finishline told me something in strictest confidence, so of course I swore all my girlfriends to absolutely secrecy before I told them. Yet somehow word got out anyway. And these were my friends! You can never tell about people."

"That's true. How are you today, Mrs. Theis?"

"I'm feeling pretty good, Doctor. We won a little something yesterday, and there is a horse in this afternoon's race that has possibilities. Finishline is at the paddock now. After we run the test lap we're going to meet for lunch at the clubhouse cafe. Would you boys care to come with us?"

"I'm fine," said Andy.

"It's too early for me also," said Lachtenslachter.

Andy watched Goldie walk away. When he was sure she was out of earshot, he said, "Doctor Lachtenslachter, is it really possible for people to make a living gambling?"

"No," said Lachtenslachter definitely. "It is not. Not if they are playing an honest game. I don't know why, but there are always people who claim they can win enough money by gambling to earn a living. If you investigate further, you always find they are making their money by doing something else, like teaching classes on how to win by gambling, or selling books about winning at gambling. You have to ask yourself why they're teaching this class or writing this book if they can make money so easily."

"What about card counting? I've heard people say you can beat the odds that way."

"You can never beat the odds in the long run, Andy. Card counting may help you win the hand. It won't let you make a profit from the game."

"Why not? If you win the hand, you win the money."

"Two words," said Lachtenslachter, holding up two fingers to demonstrate the number two. "House limits. To win at card counting you have to keep placing small bets to stay in the game until you figure out when the odds are in your favor. Then you place a really large bet. Unfortunately, the gambling houses are not run by idiots. Because of the house limits, you can't make your large bet large enough to completely win back all the money you lost on your small bets."

"Well, okay, but that's casino gambling. What about a private game of cards? Or dice, or whatever. Someplace where the house doesn't get a cut."

"If you play a tight game, and you happen to find yourself with a group of people who play fast and loose, you may very well take home their money that night. Indeed, that's why so many cardsharps prefer to hang around army bases. Soldiers are naturally reckless people who love to take chances. And they drink a lot. But if you are a careful player, word will get around and you won't be able to get up a game with anyone but other careful players. People who play loose like to play with other people who play loose."

"Hmmm." Andy leaned on the rail and watched the horses circling the track, Most of them were trotting, some were walking. Once in a while a rider would let his horse break into a brief gallop. He continued with the conversation. "It's kind of an appealing idea, to think you could travel around and make money wherever you go. You wouldn't have to be tied down to a job and one place. You could see the world without living like a vagrant. But I guess it really wouldn't work."

"I suspect that it is a lot like running away to join the circus," agreed Lachtenslachter. "It will turn out to be a lot grubbier and grimier than it appears."

"Of course, maybe there's another way."

"Really? Let me think. Have you been leading up to something, Andy?" Lachtenslachter stroked his chin, as if in deep thought. "Could you possibly be thinking of horse racing, by the merest chance? Has some combination of events suddenly put that idea into your mind?"

Andy considered the older man's words carefully. "Why is it, Doctor Lachtenslachter, that when adults say something sarcastic they don't sound nearly as sarcastic as when teenagers are being sarcastic?"

"It's the gray in our hair," the Doctor assured him. "It tends to soften our words."

"Okay, so what about horse racing? Finishline said he could pick the front runners one time out of three. Isn't that enough to make a living?"

"Regretfully, no." Lachtenslachter had little experience in the world of horse racing, and only rarely did he actually bet on games of chance. But when it came to understanding the mathematics of gambling, he was certain of his facts. "Most races are not fixed, so yes, a good handicapper can indeed spot the winners quite frequently. But the problem is that the world is full of good handicappers who are all picking the same horses. Then the odds on those horses won't be very good. When Finishline wins his one out of three times, the payoff won't be quite enough to cover those two times he lost. That's why horse gamblers are always looking for inside information. They need to know something that everyone else doesn't."

"Hmm." Andy thought about the slightly threadbare look of Finishline's trousers, and the dark edges on Goldie's jewelry, where the gold plating had worn off. If they really were living off all this, they weren't living high.

The Roan Ranger passed them again, going very fast, with Cordy clinging to its back. Lachtenslachter watched it with interest, then told Andy he had other business to attend. He wandered away just as Cordy trotted the horse up to the rail again. This time she hopped off and, to Andy's surprise, hugged him. "Hi, Cordy."

"Andy, the Roan Ranger is an excellent runner. His gait is just fine. I can't detect weakness in the front legs at all."

"I'm glad to hear it." The Roan Ranger nuzzled Andy's sleeve again, apparently searching for sugar. Andy looked around to see if anyone was watching, then patted the horse on the nose.

"He'll need training in the starting gate," Cordy continued. "We'll start that tomorrow, first thing in the morning." Although there was no one else nearby, Cordy brought her lips close to Andy's ear so she could talk to him quietly. "Andy, we did one test lap at full gallop and his time is superb! We might even beat the track record."

"Cool! Finishline and Goldie need a break."

"I held him back on the other test laps. Finishline doesn't want to attract attention to his speed, or he won't get as good odds on the race."

"Uh huh."

"Here." Cordy handed Andy the reins. "Take him for a ride."

"There's no need. I believe you."

"Not to gallop him again, silly. We'll blow him out if we run him too fast too often. Just trot him around a little bit. You're a good rider. I've seen you. Next to myself, you're the best rider in our school."

"Really? You think so?" Once again, Andy was flattered, not that Cordy thought he was a good rider, but that she had noticed him at all. "To tell the truth, I don't ride much anymore."

"It's not something you forget. At least walk him back to the stables. He likes you."

"Believe it or not, Cordy, I noticed that."

Cordy patted him on the arm. "Are you still embarrassed? I don't know why this is so important to boys. Are you worried about people seeing you ride a unicorn? They won't know."

Andy turned his head to see if Lachtenslachter was watching. The Doctor was out of sight. "Cordy, it's hard to explain."

"Then take him for a ride. I know you like to ride, Andy. Let me tell you, you won't often get a chance to ride a horse like this."

"I really shouldn't."

"Why not? Finishline won't mind." The Roan Ranger was nuzzling Andy again. "See, he wants you to ride him." Cordy showed Andy a winning smile.

He gave in. "I guess a few laps won't hurt anything."

"It's just that I don't think he thought of me as a person," Eddie told the green–eyed girl. "I was just one of his experiments. He had this great belief in the perfectibility of man. Like, you know, those politicians who think they can solve all problems if they pass enough laws. Or the teachers who think that more education is the answer to every social ill. For him, it's this science stuff. It's going to be the salvation of mankind. Better living through alchemy."

Eddie felt like an idiot saying this. Not because he said anything idiotic, or even untrue, but because he was breaking one of the cardinal rules of dating. Which was: don't talk about your feelings to girls.

Sure, lots of girls *said* they wanted you to talk about your feelings. But they didn't really mean it. They were just waiting for you to finish up so they could talk about their own feelings. When a girl asked you how you felt about something you were supposed to just say, "fine," and ask her how she felt.

It was a weeknight and he didn't have a paid show at the Blue Tune, but like the other musicians, he often came anyway to try out new material or just hang out. Weeknights weren't good for meeting babes. The ones with jobs had to get up too early in the morning to stay up late at night. The girls who went clubbing in the middle of the week did so because they were able to sleep late the next morning, which meant they had boyfriends or sugar daddies to pay their bills. Or they lived with their parents, which made things impossible.

Belatedly he said, "So how do you feel about ...?"

"Fine," the green–eyed girl said. "What does he think of your music?"

"Hah! He hates it. He didn't want me to learn the guitar. Said it drove him crazy." *Damn it*, he thought. *Why am I going on like this?* Why did he find this girl so easy to talk to?

It must be the alcohol, he decided. On nights when he was performing he only had a few drinks, and often none at all. But he wasn't playing tonight, and the green–eyed girl drank a lot. That was a good thing, because it probably would be easier to put the moves on her when the time was right. But until then he had to keep up with her, and now this was the result. He was babbling about his father. *Shut up, Eddie,* he told himself.

The green-eyed girl shifted her chair over closer to him. Close enough for her leg to rub against his. She leaned over so her breasts were almost against his chest. "Eddie," she said, "I love to listen to you *play* your music. But if I had to hear you *learn* the guitar, practicing the same chords over and over again, it would drive me crazy too. And I'm just guessing here, but there was probably more to it than just the guitar."

"Of course there was. Truth is, he wanted me to follow in his footsteps. Become a great surgeon. It was so obvious."

"But is that hard to understand? Probably ninety percent of the fathers in the world feel that way. They get over it and so do their kids."

Damn it, maybe she was right. "Maybe I was wrong," Eddie conceded. "Maybe I overreacted. I probably did. But he shouldn't have let the villagers run me out of town. He should have stood up for me."

"That's true," the green-eyed girl said. "That's pretty hard to defend. You have a point there." She looked up at him. "I know just how you feel." He thought he saw a hint of wetness in her eyes. Was she crying?

"What's your story?" he said. "Did your village run you off, too?"

The green-eyed girl looked at her glass and swirled it a little. "Sort of like that, I guess." She suddenly lifted her eyes to stare at him, then just as quickly turned her face away. When she next spoke, her voice was low and slurred. "Eddie, do you think I'm beautiful?"

"Hmm? Absolutely. Sure. No question about it."

The green-eyed girl nodded sadly. "Everyone did. That was the problem. There were so many men asking me out, bringing me gifts, buying me drinks. It was just constant temptation. And they all told me how beautiful I was, how much they loved me. You know how girls like to hear that stuff. All it took was one moment of weakness and that was it. My parents said I disgraced them. My whole village turned its back on me. Nobody threw me out, nothing like that. But I couldn't stay there."

Thank God, thought Eddie. *We're finally talking about her and not me.* Grateful to be back to the natural order of things, he said, "We all have to leave home sometime. Maybe this just gave you the push you needed."

"Yeah, maybe. Probably," said the green-eyed girl. She

reached for the bottle of wine and filled her glass half way. Eddie noticed she always filled it half way. Perhaps she thought she was drinking less that way, although he was certain she'd finish the bottle before she left. "But I'm doing all right now. I got a boyfriend, he's okay, I guess."

"Sure," said Eddie, thinking *so where is he now?*

"But what I figure, Eddie," said the green–eyed girl, "is that you ought to make up with your father."

"What?'

"Because he's probably learned a lot over the last year. I'll bet he misses you."

"To hell with that! Let him make up with me!"

"He wants to, doesn't he? He was the guy that came into the club last week, wasn't he? While you were talking with me? If he went out of his way to find this club, he must want to see you."

"Yeah, so he saw me. And we got into a fight right away."

"It wasn't that much of fight, Eddie." The girl touched his hand. "I was there. Anyway, things are different now. It's always easier to get along with your parents when you're not living with them. You can start out with short visits and slowly build up your tolerance for them, like taking allergy treatments."

Eddie thought about this. She was making a good point. Now that she brought it up, it did seem like Lachtenslachter was trying to make amends. Maybe it was Eddie's turn now. Maybe it was time to make a gesture. He said, "Did you patch things up with your parents?"

The girl did her glass swirling thing and let the light from the candle shine through the wine. "I've thought about it. It's a bit more complicated. I'd have to stop doing what I'm doing now before I could approach them. But I will. Someday."

Eddie made up his mind. "I'll send him a pass. He can get into my next show for free. We can talk between sets."

"Yes, good idea. That will give you an excuse to cut the conversation short if you start getting loud at each other."

"What the hell, it can't hurt."

"I think it's a good idea."

"And anyway," said Eddie, "he probably won't even come."

CHAPTER NINE

Not too far from the track, and not expensive at all, was an inn where many of the jockeys stayed. In the final days before the running of the Durk's Classic, it got a sudden influx of visitors from Barrenstock.

Cordy had to be close to the track in order to train the Roan Ranger. She was familiar with the place. She stayed there before because other jockeys stayed there and it gave her a chance to talk horses with them.

Finishline and Goldie had to be close to Cordy to review the training of the horse. They chose the inn because of its low prices and because the proprietor was a friend of Finishline and Goldie. He was willing to extend them credit, which few people who knew them were willing to do. Only a few days credit because, after all, he wasn't an idiot and he did know Finishline. But a few days credit was enough to see them through the race.

Lachtenslachter was able to afford something better and in fact booked himself into the Regency Hotel in the center of town, but Andy wanted to stay near the track, afraid that important decisions would be made without him if he wasn't around. Lachtenslachter acceded to his request and got him a room near the others. Now that the surgery was complete, Lachtenslachter's part in the affair was over, but he was a conscientious surgeon and visited the horse each day to conduct follow-up examinations. Andy didn't need to be there at all, but he wasn't going to miss the excitement of the race. And it took the strain off Cordy. The group needed a backup virgin to help care for the horse.

The inn was called the Horseshoe Inn. This is not a particularly imaginative name—there were a lot of inns with similar names, and every one of them had a horseshoe nailed up over the front door. But the owners of this Horseshoe Inn took the concept and ran with it. They had horseshoes—talismans of good luck—nailed up over every door, window, and mantle. They used horseshoes as door handles and candle holders. They had horseshoes on their stationary and wallpaper. There were horseshoes from famous racehorses displayed on the walls, with a few of the shoes autographed by famous jockeys. The bar sold a particularly strong drink called The Horseshoe. It had been described as the alcoholic equivalent of a kick in the head.

The Horseshoe Inn had worn carpet, worn furniture, a sagging roof, sagging floors, and sagging doors, but the bar parlor was nicely lit and warm. There you could get a pint of beer at a low price, as well as an even cheaper bowl of soup. It came with a chunk of dark brown bread. Finishline and Goldie ate at the Horseshoe Inn several times a day. In fact, once they moved in they didn't eat anywhere else, because of the low prices and because they could charge their meals to their room. They were still eating there the weekend of the Durk's Classic.

"We need to keep an eye on them," Finishline told Goldie. "It is two days until the race. After that she can do what she wants."

"They're just kids, Finishline." All good bars have a mirror behind them, so the customers can check out the rest of the people in the room without looking around and giving their actions away. The Horseshoe Inn did not have a good bar, but it had a mirror anyway. Goldie used it now to watch Cordy and Andy sitting together at a table. "We don't even know if they like each other."

"I do not know how Miss Brown feels about Andy. But I can tell you how Andy feels about Miss Brown."

"Really?" This sort of gossip was irresistible to Goldie. "Did he say something to you, Finishline?"

"He does not need to say something to me, sweetie. He is a guy and she is a doll. When a guy that age sees a doll like her, his reactions are such that any man who is not hampered by a hole in his noggin can predict the result. And this is no ordinary doll. This is a doll that goes around in riding boots and tight breeches, which is not a thing a guy is likely to see in Travaillia. Unless he goes to a certain theater of a type which is frowned upon by civic-minded citizens."

"She only wears jockey clothes when she is exercising our horse, Finishline. Most of the time she wears divided dresses. I think he's only seen her in breeches twice."

"Goldie, my sweetheart, you can trust me on this. Even if he sees her only once in jockey clothes, that is enough. Every time he looks at her from then on, his eyes are seeing divided dresses, but his mind is seeing boots, a silk blouse, and tight breeches."

"They're responsible kids, Finishline. They know what is

at stake here."

"I do not know how dolls think, Goldie. But I know how guys think. It is like what Doctor Lachtenslachter says. When a guy is with a doll, his brain is taking a vacation on a different planet."

"Does that apply to you, Finishline?"

"I am like many another guy, sweetie. You do not know this, but among the racetrack clientele, I am considered to be quite the intellectual character. Yet when I am with my ever-loving sweetheart, I am a complete chump. That is why when you ask a doll what her guy is like, she will tell you that his head is no better than a hat rack and a hat rack that is missing a few pegs at that. Even though this selfsame guy might be quite a successful operator on the street, she does not appreciate this because whenever she is near him, his brain is overheating due to the close proximity of her very self."

"Hmmm," said Goldie. She tore a piece of brown bread off a loaf and passed it to Finishline, who dunked it in his soup. "I suppose we girls have moments of weakness also. Especially when we've been drinking. Okay, Finishline. I'll keep an eye on Cordy and you keep an eye on Andy."

The two objects of their attention were sitting in a booth close to a window, with no idea that they were being scrutinized. Andy was describing to Cordy some of the scientific techniques he and Lachtenslachter used to expand the pool of knowledge, thus helping bring the benefits of modern surgery to all mankind. "You don't dig up the whole grave," he explained. "That would take too long. You just dig a hole near the headstone." He illustrated with a salt shaker to indicate a headstone and a folded napkin as the grave. "When you strike the coffin, you break it open with the point of a shovel." He tapped the napkin with the end of a spoon. "Then you drop a loop of rope down the hole and over the victim's head. Pull with all your strength, and the body slides out of the coffin and up through the hole. Fill the hole back in, pack the dirt down, and there you are. One more body to harvest for parts, and no one the wiser." He took a sip of beer. "It's best if you can get the body before it decomposes too much. Otherwise you'll just pull the head off."

Cordy took a few minutes to reflect on his story before she replied. "You know, Andy, most girls would be pretty grossed out knowing they were sitting across the table from a boy who once practiced grave robbing for a hobby. But since I spent a good deal of my youth shoveling manure, I probably am in no position to be squeamish about what other people do in their spare time."

"Weren't your parents able to hire someone to muck the stables for you?"

"Oh sure. They could have. But this was when I first got interested in horses. I had to prove I was *responsible* before they would let me have a horse of my own. At least, that was what they told me. Now I think they were just hoping that mucking the stables would persuade me to adopt a simpler, cheaper hobby, like paper dolls or needlepoint."

"I guess they changed their minds after you won the Panjandrum National."

Cordy gave a happy little laugh. "They certainly did. You know the best part? It was my father's idea. It was just a publicity stunt for his business. He didn't think for a second that I'd actually win. At the end I was supposed to take off my cap and let my long hair tumble down, and everyone in the stands was supposed to say, 'Ooo, it's a girl jockey!' My Mom didn't even go to the race. I wish you could have seen her expression when I brought home the trophy."

"I was wondering about that? What's with the short hair?" Andy had never seen a girl with short hair.

"Easier to keep clean. You can get awfully dirty riding."

Although Travaillia was a place where teenagers could get alcohol if they wanted it, they were drinking small beer, which contained but a trace of it. "I still have to drink Durk's," Cordy explained to Andy, "Even though I'm mad at them for pulling me out of their race. I'm still under contract to them, and this is part of my contract."

"Um, right," said Andy, who thought they had been drinking fizzy water. "Who is that guy?"

"Who?"

"That guy at the bar you've been looking at."

Cordy made a pretense of looking around the room. There were a half dozen other men there, mostly jockeys and trainers. One of the jockeys was on crutches. He was leaning against the bar, trying to chat up the barmaid. Standing a little apart from them both was a young man in very expensive clothes.

This was Waxroth's henchman Lancet. He was tall and slender, with piercing blue eyes and glossy dark hair that had a slight natural wave to it. Every ruffle on his silk shirt was perfectly pressed. Every button on his exquisitely tailored jacket was gleaming silver, as were the buckles on his highly polished shoes. He stood with easy grace, one elbow resting on the scarred wooden bar, one foot on the brass rail, and he watched Cordy in the mirror.

"I don't know him," said Cordy. "He just caught my eye."

"Yeah," said Andy. "Nice clothes." He felt a sudden, slight, sinking, hollowness. He was smart enough to recognize this feeling as jealousy, and also smart enough to know he shouldn't show it. He slid out of the booth. "I guess I'll see you in the morning."

"What? Where are you going?"

"Finishline and I are going to take turns sitting up with the Roan Ranger. He has so much at stake in this horse that he doesn't want to leave it unguarded. So I told him I'd take turns with him."

"Oh. That's nice of you. I'll take a turn also."

Andy shook his head. "We thought you might say that. But you need to get your sleep. You're the jockey, and the trainer, so you have to be fresh, alert, perky, at the top of your form and all that sort of stuff."

"I guess that's true. If I don't get a good night's sleep my perkiness level drops considerably."

"And we can't allow that. So I'll see you later."

Cordy watched him walk to the other table and talk briefly with Finishline. The two men left, while Goldie picked up her glass and brought it over to Cordy's table. "I see you have an admirer."

Cordy looked at the handsome boy in the nice clothes. He flashed her a bright smile. She looked away, a little embarrassed. She had attracted a lot of male admirers since her big win in the Grand Panjandrum, but she hadn't yet gotten used to the attention. Still, she might have been tempted to flirt with him, if Goldie had not casually moved over and seated herself across from Cordy. Cordy gave a mental shrug. The boy wasn't looking at her anyway. She chatted with Goldie for a while, but the next time she looked over at the bar, the boy was gone.

She saw him again when she went to her room. The Horseshoe Inn had three floors, with a dozen guest rooms on the second floor. The first floor was given over to public rooms, while the third floor housed the staff and servants. Cordy left Goldie in the bar parlor and went up the stairs with a large brass room key in one hand and a wrought iron candle holder in the other. She had stayed at this inn many times before, and knew that normally a lamp burned on a small table at the end of the hall. Tonight the lamp was out and the hall was dark. In the gloom she could make out someone crouched near her door. She approached him cautiously, her candle held in front of her, her other hand firmly gripping the heavy brass key, ready to strike if trouble arose.

But as she got closer she was able to make out the handsome young man she had seen earlier in the bar. He looked up as she approached and his boyish face lit in a smile. "Hello," he said.

"Hello."

He seemed glad to see her and said so. "Could I trouble you for a light? My candle went out and I can't find my room number."

Cordy came close enough to see that he was kneeling over a dead candle in an iron candle holder, identical to the holder she carried. Bits and pieces from a tinderbox were arrayed on the floor, but apparently he did not have a good flint and wasn't getting sparks from it. She bent down to light his candle from her own. "No problem."

"Thanks." He rose with her. The top of her head came to his chin. She had to look up. His silver buttons glittered. Candlelight danced in his eyes. He had the nicest eyes, she decided. He said, "You look familiar. Have I seen you before?"

"I was downstairs in the bar-parlor."

"Yes, I saw you. But even then you looked familiar. Are you Corduroy Brown, the famous jockey?"

Automatically Cordy put a hand back to pat her hair. She hadn't been a celebrity long enough to grow tired of being recognized. She certainly did not object when it brought her to the attention of fine looking boys. "Yes, thanks for recognizing me."

"I saw you race. You were awesome. You know, my whole family drinks Durk's beer because of you."

I'm sorry, Cordy almost said. Aloud she said, "I'm very flattered. Perhaps you'll see me race again this Sunday."

His smile tightened, showing a little bit more of his teeth, giving his mouth a slightly feral appearance. He said, "Perhaps not. May I walk you to your door?"

"My door is right here." Cordy turned the knob. "Well, good night."

He put his hand on hers. A little thrill went through her. "I'm so pleased that we were able to meet. I'd like to ask you a few questions. Would you mind if I came in for a minute?"

It took Cordy a few seconds to get over her surprise. She looked into his innocent, smiling, handsome face, and almost agreed. Then common sense returned to her. "Into my room? At night? Certainly not. You are very forward." She stepped inside and started closing the door. But to make sure she had not offended him, she turned around and said, "But if you want to see me again, I'll be at ..."

Her words were cut off when he gave the door a massive kick. It slammed into her shoulder, knocked her off balance, and sent her candle spinning to the floor. Inside a second he stepped into the dark room, seized her arm with one hand, and closed the door with the other. All done smoothly, gracefully, and very fast.

Cordy was stunned by the sudden violence, but still managed to break free and back away from her assailant. He caught up to her, grabbed both shoulders, shook her once, and shoved her onto the bed. She sucked in her breath to scream. He anticipated that, too. He put one hand around her throat and squeezed. "Now," he said. "We could do this the hard way. Or we could do it the easy way. You could cooperate with me and not get hurt. Unfortunately for you, I've already decided we're going to do it the hard way."

Cordy clawed at his arms, but her short nails were ineffective against his thick coat. She reached for his face, but he batted her hands away. Still gripping her throat, he pushed her down into the ticking. Her lungs strained for air. He grabbed her blouse at the collar and ripped it down to her waist.

"Great!" said a voice behind him.

Centuries ago, in a remote area of the Far East, a boy grew up in the tiny village of Ah Tum. His name was Jin Go. The truth of his life has been lost to time and repetition, but the legends of Jin Go are known to any practitioner of *Noh Kandu*.

The legends tell us that Jin Go's family was the largest landowner in the area surrounding Ah Tum, and thus Jin Go was born into a life of comfortable means. Yet he grew up with the knowledge that gold was mere dross if you do not have your health, for Jin Go suffered all through his boyhood from headaches, nausea, shortness of breath, and physical weakness. His parents consulted physicians and herbalists, who scratched their heads, consulted each other, and prescribed many powders. But nothing they did helped, and Jin Go grew from a skinny and sickly child to a skinny and sickly young man. Then a traveler to the village brought a strange tale.

He told of a tropical island called Kah Pree, fronted by golden sand on one end, and on the other, a mountain of sheer cliffs that overlooked the sea. On these cliffs the monks of Kah Pree had built their monastery, and here they practiced a mystical system of exercise and meditation, by which a man could directly access his qi—his inner strength—to achieve serenity and physical well-being. Jin Go's family questioned the stranger for three days until they were satisfied that his story was true. Then they sent Jin Go with an offering to the monastery and a respectful request for help.

His entourage traveled for long months, crossing mountains, deserts, and rivers, and having many adventures that do not concern us here, before reaching the island of Kah Pree. Arriving at the monastery on his gilded palanquin, Jin Go prostrated himself before the Abbott. He promised he would renounce worldly goods and dedicate his life to meditation and service if the monks could cure his ills. The Abbott looked Jin Go over for a long time, listened to his story, stroked his long white beard pensively, and finally told Jin Go that his symptoms would disappear if he'd stop using so much MSG in his cooking. But, the Abbott continued, as long as Jin Go was here he could take advantage of a special offer for their exercise and meditation system. If he paid for a year's membership in advance he could get an additional two more months free, plus the co-ed exercise class on Tuesday and Thursday nights, and unrestricted use of the weight room and jacuzzi. However, Jin Go had to decide right away, because this offer was only available to first time visitors. Thus did Jin Go join the monastery of Kah Pree.

Month after month Jin Go faithfully spent every evening at the monastery. Diligently he studied the techniques and philosophy of *Noh Kandu*, toning his body, calming his mind, and learning how to focus and control his qi. He spent his days hanging out at the beach on the other side of the island, working on his tan. It was there that he first saw the love of his life, the beautiful Ki Ten.

A moment later he decided to renounce his monastic vows of chastity, self-denial, and celibacy. Okay, in all truth he never really intended to keep those vows very long, and in fact had crossed his fingers while making them. But so far he hadn't actually broken them. Now he was ready. For one look at Ki Ten's almond eyes, her soft lashes, her full lips, her flawless skin, and her totally knockout figure, and his own heart was forever lost.

Jin Go was contemplating trying out some lines on her when his reverie was interrupted. A local hoodlum, a jerk known named Bah Dghai, the 'bully of the beach', kicked sand in his face. Bah Dghai had done this many times before, but for the first time Jin Go decided he wasn't going to take it lying down. He rose to his full height. Then he rose two inches above his full height. Bah Dghai had grabbed Jin Go's collar and lifted him off the ground.

In a strangled voice, Jin Go attempted to tell Bah Dghai what he thought of him. Bah Dghai laughed scornfully. "Listen, twerp. I'd punch you in the face except ... um." Bah Dghai paused while he tried to think of a reason why he shouldn't punch a random harmless beachgoer in the face. Nothing came to him, so he clobbered Jin Go several times and left him bleeding face down in the sand.

Jin Go regained consciousness to the sound of Ki Ten's soft, musical voice. "Don't worry about it, ramen arms," she said. He raised his head in time to see her step over him and pass to Bah Dghai a slip of rice paper, on which she had scribbled her name, home address, and the locations of several bars where she liked to hang out. For good measure she drew little hearts around her name.

Deeply humiliated, Jin Go returned to his austere cell in the monastery. He wrote a letter to his father, expressing the shame he felt for his family, for his village, and for himself. He explained that he would not return to his village. Instead he intended to immerse himself in meditation and the study of *Noh Kandu*.

For half a year he did exactly that, until one day a courier arrived with a package from Ah Tum. Inside was a scroll from his father. It explained to Jin Go exactly what he had to do to regain his self-respect and achieve his dreams.

Jin Go wasted no time. The very next day he returned to the beach. Nothing had changed. Warm waves still lapped at the shore. Seabirds still wheeled overhead. Tiny crabs skittered over the hot white sand. Under the noon sun, Ki Ten's body gleamed with oil. She lay on a cotton towel, her long, dark hair spread about her. Jin Go thought she looked more beautiful than ever. Next to her, Bah Dghai looked as tough as ever.

Yet Jin Go did not hesitate. Without showing a trace of

fear, he boldly walked up to Bah Dghai and kicked sand in his face.

A second later Bah Dghai was on his feet, his fingers curled into claws, ready to wrap around Jin Go's throat. But Jin Go responded with lightning quickness. In one fast, fluid movement, a motion almost too quick to register on the human brain, he reached inside his tunic and whipped out a diamond bracelet.

It had arrived in the same box as the scroll from his father. The diamonds glittered, hard and bright in the noonday sun. But not half so hard and bright as the glitter in Ki Ten's eyes. Without a moment's hesitation she dealt Bah Dghai three quick blows to the head, chest, and midsection. The bully's eyes rolled back in his head and he dropped, unconscious, to the sand. A second later Ki Ten had molded herself to Jin Go's side.

"My love for you is as abundant as the water of the sea that surrounds us, and flows from my heart like the hot sun meeting the sand," she told him, snapping the bracelet out of his hands and fastening it around her wrist. "So what's your name, big boy?"

"Jin Go," Jin Go told her. "Say, that was totally awesome." He indicated the bully lying on the sand. "Where did you learn to fight like that?"

"I took an exercise course at that monastery up on the mountain. Something called *Noh Kandu*."

"Really? I'm studying *Noh Kandu*."

"Yeah, it's great, Jin Go. The monks think it's all about meditation and learning to control your qi. Nonsense like that. But, I'll let you in on a secret, my love. If you do the movements really fast, it makes a great martial art."

"Hmm," said Jin Go thoughtfully. That very night, while strolling along the beach in the moonlight, he made a proposal to Ki Ten. She agreed to his plan. With a loan from Jin Go's father, they licensed the *Noh Kandu* system from the monastery, sold a bunch of martial arts franchises, collected big bucks, and lived happily ever after. Over the centuries the teachers of their system spread their knowledge throughout the east and a few of them even ventured overseas.

Nonetheless, only a handful of people in Travaillia had heard of *Noh Kandu*.

Lancet turned. The door was open again, and Andy was coming through it. "This is great!" he said again. "Every guy wants to rescue a pretty girl from danger. But how many of us ever get to do it? Now, here's my chance."

"Get lost, kid. This isn't for you."

Andy's arms were at his side, but his fists were clenched. "The door is open. Now is your chance to leave."

Lancet shoved Cordy away. She backed against the wall, clutching her throat. His hand went to his pocket and came out holding a wicked little knife with a bone handle. "You're annoying me, kid. If you make me cut you, I'll cut her too. Because I do that sort of thing when I'm angry."

He didn't have time to say more. An effective knife block requires two hands, but Andy decided he could risk a cut. He came forward with three small, dance-like steps, almost too quick to see. One hand chopped across the inside of Lancet's arm, knocking the knife aside, while the other slammed across the bridge of Lancet's nose. It was a movement called the Swimming Aardvark—no one knew why— and it left the would-be rapist stunned. Before he could react Andy hit him again in the throat, while seizing his wrist in the Mother of Lobsters grip and twisting it so Lancet was forced to let go of his knife. It stuck, point down, into the floor.

Lancet didn't give up easily. He dropped to the floor himself and swung his legs, kicking Andy's ankles out from under him. Andy landed on his back. Lancet grabbed his knife and scrambled to his feet, only to find that Andy had already bounced back up by propelling himself with his elbows and shoulders, a movement called the Lizard Returns to the Rock. Before he could raise his knife Andy danced in, kicked him in the knee, and jumped back again. It was a precision martial arts movement that his sensei referred to as Kicking Your Opponent in the Knee. It is a tricky move. Not many fighters can target a moving opponent exactly in the kneecap. Even fewer can keep fighting after receiving a kick to the kneecap. The blow left Lancet swearing and limping. He was tough, though. He still made good time as he hobbled out the door and disappeared down the darkened hall.

"Are you all right?"

"Fine," Cordy said. And she was fine, a bit shook up, but no real damage. She opened her mouth to thank Andy for coming to her aid, but to her own surprise, the words that came out were, "I didn't let him in."

"What?"

"That man. He forced his way into my room. I didn't invite

him in." For reasons she couldn't explain, it had become important to Cordy that Andy didn't think she was dating anyone.

"Sure," said Andy. "I didn't think you did."

"Anyway, thank you. You showed up just in time."

"Finishline sent me back with some questions about tomorrow's training." Andy looked at the door with satisfaction. "That was great. After all those years of studying *Noh Kandu*, I finally got to try it out. My sensei was right. Give your opponent a means to escape. Do not give yourself a chance to escape."

"That's deep, Andy."

"Yeah. My sensei likes to ramble on about the moral issues of fighting." Andy smacked a fist into his palm. "He insists that his art should only be used to defend yourself against an attacker, never to attack someone yourself. In fact, even if he is attacked, a true master of *Noh Kandu* will always seek to avoid confrontation."

"That's very wise, I'm sure. Is that the way you truly feel?"

"Hell, no! Maybe we students have to act conciliatory, because it's the right thing to do, but deep inside we're always hoping the enemy will attack anyway, so we can kick his head in."

"Yes, I'm pretty sure I'd feel the same way." Cordy put her arms around Andy's waist. "I am really grateful, Andy. And you looked very cool doing your fight movements."

"I did, didn't I?" Andy flexed his muscles a bit. "And he was bigger than me, too. Don't you think he was bigger than me?"

"Maybe a little. He was taller."

"So he had a longer reach. And he was armed with a knife. Yeah, I think I did pretty well."

"I agree you were very heroic."

"I don't suppose you want to do it again, do you?"

"What?"

"Well, maybe you could walk down a dark alley and see if anyone jumps you, and then I could clobber him."

"I think you've been heroic enough for one night." Cordy kissed him. "I will be sure to tell everyone tomorrow." She kissed him again. "But now, Andy, you are in my room. And you are a boy and I am a girl. And that is the sort of thing that starts rumors. So I think you need to go back to your own room. And I need to go to bed. One more kiss and off you go."

Andy tried to make the kiss linger, but Cordy was firm and kept the gesture semi-chaste. Then she gently propelled him toward the door. She did, in fact, consider giving him another kiss at the doorway, but when she pulled it open, she was surprised to find a man standing there. So was Andy. It was a very big man, a man with a broken nose and knuckles the size of walnuts, wearing a slouch hat and a lumpy suit. He looked at Cordy, then looked over her head, into the darkened room. He saw Andy and nodded to him. He was polite, but when he spoke his voice had the grinding quality of a millstone. He said, "Excuse me. Miss Brown? Miss Corduroy Brown?"

Cordy nodded.

"Thanks," he said, and took her arm in two big fists and calmly broke it.

CHAPTE TEN

Lachtenslachter had spent many years practicing medicine before he retired to pursue research, and old habits die hard. It was still difficult for him to see an injured person without feeling an overwhelming desire to make him sit in a waiting room for several hours and fill out forms. On the positive side, at least for Cordy, was that Lachtenslachter didn't feel comfortable traveling without at least his small medical bag, which carried a basic assortment of instruments, bandages, and ointments. It did not have plaster, but he sent Andy to wake up the owner of a nearby apothecary and procure some. Leeches, the Doctor thought, could probably wait until morning.

By the time Andy was back with medical supplies, Lachtenslachter was dressed and ready to go. It was not soon enough for Andy, who did his best to hurry him along the dark streets to the Horseshoe Inn. Lachtenslachter was more concerned with Andy. "I'm fine. My back is fine. We need to get to Cordy."

"You don't look fine."

"It's just bruises. His face had already swollen before Andy reached the Regency Hotel, and now the bruises were turning black. "He only punched me in the face. Come on, Dr. Lachtenslachter. We're wasting time." He tried to hurry the Doctor through the dark streets.

"Andy, you know that was a foolish thing to do."

"I know."

"*Noh Kandu* is an excellent exercise system and it may be a fine martial art. But it's totally useless against a man who is twice your size."

"I know."

"You can't take on everyone. No martial art is effective against someone who is more than thirty percent heavier than you are. That's merely physics. That's why martial art competitions have weight divisions."

"I know, I know, *I know*. My sensei went over it again and again. But that man broke her arm! What was I supposed to do, just stand there?"

"The intelligent thing to do is to run away and summon

help. I know your sensei taught you that." Lachtenslachter sighed. "But I suppose it really is too much to expect a man to abandon a woman in distress. I wouldn't have done it at your age either."

They reached the door of the Horseshoe Inn. Andy hustled Lachtenslachter up the stairs to Cordy's room. Cordy lay on her bed, looking very pale, with Finishline, Goldie, and the innkeeper standing around her looking very worried. A basin of hot water stood on the night table. Goldie had already finished sponging off Cordy's arm.

Lachtenslachter's eyes lit up when he saw her.

"The right arm!" he enthused. "This is your lucky day, Miss Brown! I have a perfect replacement. We just need to get you back to my laboratory. Now it won't be a pleasant journey, but I have some painkillers here that will ease the ..."

"What!" said Andy. "It's a broken arm! Just splint it, Doctor Lachtenslachter."

Lachtenslachter waved his hand casually. "There's no need to repair it when it can be replaced for only slightly more cost. I have an arm that is in excellent condition, a real find. I've been saving it for just such an opportunity."

"I don't think Cordy wants ..."

"Wait until you see it, Miss Brown. Perfect skin, long slender fingers, a nice tan. It's a real beauty. You'll love it."

"She doesn't need a new arm, Doctor Lachtenslachter. Just fix this one."

"At least take a look at it. You owe it to yourself ..."

"Doctor Lachtenslachter!"

"I really think that I prefer to keep this arm, Doctor Lachtenslachter," Cordy said weakly.

"But if you insist, I can splint this arm," said Lachtenslachter. He explored the injury with experienced fingers. "Multiple fracture, hmmm. Rather serious, I'm afraid. You're sure you wouldn't rather—very well. Just inhale from this bottle, please. This will dull the pain—feel better now? Good. Bite down on this wad of cloth, please. Good. Now I'm going to set the bones and this may hurt a little ..." There was a slight grinding noise that made everyone in the room wince except Cordy. "And there we are. That wasn't so bad, was it? And now the bandages, Andy." Andy passed him the strips of linen cloth soaked in plaster. In a remarkably short time the arm was stitched, splinted, bandaged, cast, and suspended by Cordy's side in a sling made from a pillowcase the innkeeper donated. A half hour later she was sitting up, another hour after that she was back in the bar parlor eating soup with her left hand. No one felt like sleeping tonight.

"Good job, Doctor Lachtenslachter," Andy told his mentor. "Thanks."

"Nothing to it, Andy. Now if we had a good storm and a couple of lightning rods, I could have really ..."

"Yes, yes," Andy interrupted, "but I'm sure she appreciates it just the way it is."

Finishline took Andy and Lachtenslachter aside. "You know, Doc, I hear stories sometimes about jockeys who ride even with broken bones ..."

They both gave him severe looks.

"... although I am sure that it is not wise in this particular situation," Finishline finished morosely.

"That arm won't even have time to set well before the Durk's Classic, much less heal," said Lachtenslachter. "If she takes a fall, and the ends of the bone rub together ..."

Finishline winced. "Ouch. Okay, Doctor, I see your point. It hurts just to think about it."

Across the room Cordy was talking to Goldie. "I think I can do it," she said. "There's still one day to give the bones time to set. Jockeys break bones all the time. They tape them up and ride anyway."

"I know. It's their job and they need the money. They don't win, though."

"Sure they do. Lots of them."

"Yeah? Name some."

Cordy was silent for several minutes. She scraped her spoon around the inside of the bowl a few times before losing interest in it. Eventually she said, "I should have been more careful."

"Don't blame yourself, Cordy. We both know who is behind this."

"I should have suspected something. I've always had bad luck with boys. My last boyfriend was a werewolf."

In a country other than Travaillia, a statement like this would have provoked skepticism. Goldie merely said, "Bad experience, huh?"

"He told me that he loved me. He said he'd never do anything to hurt me. I trusted him. And then came the full moon."

"What happened?"

"He was arrested down at the zoo, trying to make it with the lioness. Two timing jerk."

Goldie patted her shoulder. "Relax, Cordy. You've had a hard night. Now it's time to get some sleep. Do you want the Doctor to give you something for the pain?"

"No, I'm fine as long as I don't move it. What will you do, Goldie? What will you and Finishline do?"

"We'll get by. Our luck will turn around. It always turns around. Tomorrow we'll withdraw the Roan Ranger from the race. We'll get some of that registration fee back. Not all of it, but enough to give us a bit of a stake. With the right race and good odds, we'll be back on our feet in no time."

It was the most unconvincing little speech Cordy had ever heard. Her thoughts must have showed in her face, for Goldie gave her a wan smile and changed the subject. "You know what that cast needs? A little decoration. Come with me. Let's see if we can put some sparklies on it."

Cordy followed her up to her room. Finishline's worn suits were hanging on hooks. They seemed to fit right in with the threadbare decor of the place. Goldie opened a battered trunk and produced an equally battered jewelry box. It had clearly been very expensive when new, but the clasp was bent, and the mother-of-pearl inlay had been chipped and not repaired. Goldie rummaged through it, setting aside the bracelets. "They won't fit around the cast." She opted instead for a string of faux pearls. "If we wrap this three times around your wrist, like so." She stood back and surveyed her handiwork.

"It looks nice," Cordy offered. She didn't have much jewelry of her own, being too young to have acquired much, and also having more of an interest in horses than clothes. When she needed jewelry she borrowed it from her mother.

"No," said Goldie. "The white on white isn't showy enough." She removed the pearls and substituted a silver-plated chain. "Oh yes. Much better."

Cordy looked down at her arm, then moved over to the looking glass so she could see herself. She had to admit that the sparkling silver metal did add a touch of glamour to her appearance. She couldn't resist looking into Goldie's box to see what else was there. "Goldie? What are all the slips of paper?"

Goldie took the box from her. "These? These are my most precious jewels." She drew a slip of paper out of the box. "A girl has to have good jewelry, you know. There's nothing like a nice diamond to show that a girl has class. If it's good quality. Cordy, I really think you need to take the winnings from your next race and get yourself a pair of earrings. Nothing gaudy, you understand. Something quiet and tasteful. The point is to accent your own beauty, not draw attention to the jewelry itself."

Cordy looked at the slip. "Is this a pawn ticket?"

"Well, I'm going to redeem it someday. This is a pair of diamond earrings that my first husband gave me. Only quarter carat, in fourteen carat gold studs. Don't buy first class diamonds for your ears, because they don't show enough. But try to get fourteen carat gold settings, because they have the most variety and it's easier to find pieces that match. Anyway, Finishline and I made an investment in a horse named Alabaster Moonlet. She turned out not to run so well, but we plan to redeem that ticket pretty soon now."

Goldie selected another pawn ticket from the jewelry box. "An emerald pendant. This is where you put your best stones. Especially after you develop some cleavage." She held the ticket to her breast.

"Um, right," said Cordy. Under ordinary circumstances she had enough snap to recognize when a conversation was going badly, and would have changed the subject at that point, but her mind was still a bit foggy from the painkillers. She picked another slip of paper from the box. "What is this?"

Goldie took it from her. "These are my best pearls. Every girl needs a strand of pearls. Your most basic outfit is a little black dress and strand of pearls. These were a gift from an elderly gentlemen back when I was still ... um ... dancing. I could have sold them for a lot of money, but I could never bear to part with them. So I pawned them instead. It was a nice little shop right near the track at Pumello. Very convenient."

"I think ... I think I should go to bed now," said Cordy, looking for an exit, both from the room and the conversation.

"Of course, honey. I'm sorry I kept you up. Oh, let me show you this first." Goldie presented her with another pawn ticket. Cordy couldn't help but notice the date. The ticket was six years old. "It's for a ring?"

"A diamond ring. Cordy, wait until you see it. It's beautiful. Finishline gave it to me. We had a big win on the fifth race at Saragasso, and that very evening he gave it to me at dinner. It's my engagement ring." Goldie closed her eyes and twisted the paper around her ring finger, a rapturous expression on her face as she relived the event. "I was so happy I cried. He even got down on one knee when he presented it to me. I swore to Finishline that I would never take it off. And

I never did, for three whole weeks, until we needed the money to invest on a four-year-old mare at the Viaduct. We promised each other that this will be the first ticket we redeem when we build up our stake."

Sometimes you hear a story, Cordy decided, that is made even sadder by the knowledge that the woman telling it doesn't realize she's telling a sad story. She left Goldie putting away her box of pawn shop tickets and hurried to Andy's room. He wasn't in it, nor was he in the bar-parlor downstairs. She did a quick check of the public rooms, but couldn't find him at all. That meant, she concluded after a moment's thought, that he had either accompanied Doctor Lachtenslachter back to his own hotel, or had gone to stand guard over the Roan Ranger. She was about to head over to the track when she saw Andy returning from the direction of Lachtenslachter's hotel. "Finishline advised me," he told her when he got closer, "to get some sleep. He said there is no point standing guard over the horse when we don't have anyone to ride him. Although I don't think Finishline is getting any sleep himself."

Cordy grabbed his arm with her good hand. "Andy," she said desperately, "you've got to ride him."

"What? Ride the Roan Ranger?"

"Yes, the Roan Ranger! Is there any other horse we both know about?"

"No, it was a rhetorical question, I guess. You surprised me. I needed time to collect my thoughts."

Cordy waited an entire two seconds. "Are they collected now?"

"No. You want me to ride the Roan Ranger in the Durk's Classic? Okay, now my thoughts are collected."

"Andy, the Roan Ranger has to run in this race. You're the only one who can do it."

"No, I can't. Really."

"Sure you can. You're an excellent rider. The Durk's Classic is open to amateur jockeys. And the Roan Ranger trusts you."

"Cordy, I can gallop a horse around a track. That doesn't mean I can race him."

"You've competed in gymkhanas, the same as me. And you always did well in those. I've seen you."

"Gymkhana isn't flat racing, Cordy. I'll be going up against professional jockeys. The odds of winning are tiny."

"The odds of winning are zero if the horse doesn't run. I

know it's a long shot, Andy, but Finishline and Goldie need the Roan Ranger to run in this race."

"Well, I can't do it. Cordy, I'm sure there are other jockeys who can ride the Roan Ranger."

"It's a big world. You're right, there probably are plenty of other jockeys who can ride the Roan Ranger. Somewhere. But we don't know who they are or where they are and we've only got one day."

Andy would have thrown up his hands in exasperation, if Cordy had not been gripping one arm. "There will be other races, Cordy. The horse isn't going anywhere. Your arm will heal before the end of the season. And if not, there is always next year."

"I don't think there's going to be another season for them, Andy. You know they can't afford to feed and stable a horse for a year. They have their backs to the wall, Andy, I know it. I think they're in real trouble."

Andy remembered something Finishline had told him the first day they met, something about Waxroth's tendency to combine business acumen with grievous bodily injury. Reluctantly, he mentioned this to Cordy. She nodded. "That's Werner Waxroth, all right."

"Damn it, Cordy. I don't like it when people lay guilt trips on me. Especially girls, for some reason. It's unfair. You make it sound like their lives are in my hands."

"If it sounds that way, maybe that's because it is that way. Andy, what do you think is going to happen to them?"

"If they're in trouble, they got themselves in trouble." Andy immediately regretted saying this. It was callous, even to his own ears. Of course he didn't want his friends to get hurt.

"Did they?" Cordy looked at him speculatively. "Get themselves into trouble, I mean? Did someone else help them along? Didn't someone persuade Doctor Lachtenslachter to go along with ..."

"Ouch. Okay, okay. I was trying to help them."

"Help them some more. We've got to try, at least. Even if you come in third there will be some money."

"Aaagh!" Andy shook her hand off his arm, and ran his fingers through his hair. "Yeah, okay. I'm in. I'm in, already. I'll do it. You don't have to go on about it."

Cordy took hold of a collar button and pulled his face down to her own. "Thank you."

"On the other hand, if you're going to kiss me, you can go on about it a bit more."

"I'll save you some for afterward."

"Just one more thing," said Andy. "Don't tell Doctor Lachtenslachter I'm riding in a race. Because I don't want him to worry about me. So don't say anything. Okay?

"I thought I made myself clear on this," said Waxroth. "I said quite distinctly that I did not want you to break her arm. What part of 'no broken arms' did you not understand?"

"It seemed like a good idea at the time," said Grogan mildly. He did not let Diana give him a drink this time, since he was being chastised, and he wanted to seem like he was taking it seriously.

"Well it wasn't a good idea. You're getting into a rut, Grogan. What is it with you and broken arms?"

"Arms are the best. You can't do kneecaps. Sure, they're painful, but they're permanent. A broken kneecap is for life. Once you've done the kneecaps, you got no place to go. You have to save your kneecappings for people you want to make a permanent example of."

"I didn't ask for a kneecap."

"I don't object to kneecaps, mind you. I like kneecaps. I just don't want to talk you into a kneecapping when a kneecapping wouldn't suit your needs."

"Grogan, I didn't call you in to hear a discourse on the philosophy of thuggery."

As a rule, Grogan was not known for sparkling conversation, but now he was on his favorite subject. He kept going. "Hips are nearly as bad. It takes a skilled sawbones to reset a hip. Chances are your client can't afford that kind of medical skill. If he did he wouldn't be one of your clients. So without expensive surgery, you end up with another permanent cripple."

"What about broken ribs?" asked Waxroth, in spite of himself.

"Not worth it, Boss. You grab a guy, you give him a bear hug, you try to crush his ribs, the chances are good you'll end up breaking his spine. So how can he pay you back if he's paralyzed and can't work? If you do break only the ribs, it's not a disabling injury. Not for a jockey. Half the guys riding out there have taped up ribs. So it's too much risk for too little gain."

"Okay, how about a broken jaw? You can't tell me that a broken jaw isn't painful. It's humiliating, too. He can still work, but he's going around for months with his jaw wired shut, drinking his meals through a straw. Now that's a lesson he won't unlearn."

"It's not humiliating enough, Boss. Once he can talk again, he'll tell people he got in a bar fight. He'll make himself seem like a tough guy. He might even say he beat the other guy up even worse. I'm telling you, Boss, nothing proves your point like a good broken arm."

"I suppose I shouldn't even ask, but what about a broken leg?"

Grogan looked pained. "There's no artistry to breaking a leg."

"Spare me." Waxroth selected a cigar from a box, but didn't light it. Instead he tapped it on the desk while he thought. "Anyway, what's done is done, and there's going to be hell to pay. I want you to keep a low profile for the next week or two. Take a vacation out of town. And take that idiot kid Lancet with you. How's he doing, anyway?"

"He hurts a lot."

"Good. Serves him right. I gave him the plum job of violating an innocent, helpless girl and he screwed it up. At least we got that damn horse out of the race."

"No, Boss. It's still in."

"What? Last I heard they were asking for the registration fee back."

"They got another jockey, just like I said." Grogan looked mystified. "Boss, why are you so surprised? Of course they got another jockey. Why wouldn't they?"

"Who's the jockey?"

"Some new kid. Andrew something. An amateur. In fact, the same kid who kicked Lancet's butt last night. Tough kid. If I'd known he was riding I'd have worked him over a bit more."

"What was he doing there?"

"I don't know, Boss. He must be a friend of National Cordy.

"Not friendly enough, damn it," muttered Waxroth.

"What was that, Boss? I didn't hear you."

"Never mind. Where is he staying?"

"Same inn as the girl and Finishline. I've been keeping tabs for you. Right after breakfast, Finishline took him down to the jockey club and got him registered."

"Damn it all to hell." Waxroth looked at his cigar, decided it was too early, and put in back in the box. "All right, Grogan, that's all for now. Draw some cash, take Lancet, and put him on a coach out of town. Tell him to hole up somewhere for a month. You too, as soon as the race is over. Stick around for now, but stay out of sight."

"Sure, Boss."

"I'm going to stop this kid from riding."

"You want me to break ...?"

"No! Get moving!"

Waxroth bent over his desk. When he heard Grogan open the door he yelled, "Diana!" without looking up. He still didn't look up when he heard her come back into the room, which was a shame, because the men who did look at Diana that morning had enjoyed the sight. She was wearing high-heeled boots of thin leather that hugged her calves and made her already long legs seem even longer. A long, tight, black dress, in a clingy soft fabric, was slit along the side, all the way up to her hip, and showed that her black stockings stopped mid-thigh and no slip or petticoat came down to meet them. A halter top molded the front of the dress tight against her breasts, but the back plunged nearly to her waist, leaving bare an expanse of smooth skin to provide contrast for a tumble of long red hair. She carried a tiny, black, beaded clutch purse, which she set on the sideboard while she poured herself a drink. Then sat down herself in the chair Grogan had just vacated. When Waxroth finally did look at her she gave him what she thought was her sultriest smile.

Waxroth looked her up and down, in a way that he had done the day he hired her to be his personal assistant. He hadn't looked at her like that since, so she felt a light glow of achievement that she had finally rekindled his interest.

"You look beautiful," Waxroth said.

About time, she thought. "Thank you, Werner. You really like this dress?"

"The dress suits you very well. And I like what you've done with your hair."

Better and better. "Oh I just teased it a bit to give it a little more body. I'm so glad you like it."

"It's the kind of look that all men like," said Waxroth. "You might change your lipstick to something a bit brighter, though. Bright red, or hot pink. Also your nail polish. Do you have bright red?"

"Um, sure Werner." Diana thought the makeup she was wearing was eye-catching enough, perhaps too much so. But if Werner wanted bright red, she was ready to give it to him. "I'm glad you're finally telling me things like this, Werner. I could do so much for you if you'd tell me what you like." She moved closer to him and put her hand over his. Impatiently he pulled away.

"It's not what I like that is important tonight, Diana. It's what teenage boys like. They go for the trashy look."

Diana did not respond immediately. The clock on the wall ticked quietly for nearly a minute. Her pretty lips tightened. Waxroth dipped his quill and wrote out instructions on a slip of paper. He was just about finished when Diana said, very carefully, "Werner, honey, you didn't mean to say that I look trashy, did you?"

"If you don't, then you need to change. Buy a new dress if you have to. Maybe something leather. They like leather. Whatever it takes. You know what teenage boys want better than I do."

"There is nothing wrong with the way I look. I certainly do not look—wait—why should I care how teenage boys look at me?"

"Because you're going out with one tonight."

"I thought *we* were going out tonight. To a show. We have tickets."

"Change of plans." Waxroth handed her a slip of paper. "This kid is riding in tomorrow's race. Here is his name, a description, and the inn where he's staying. Find him and take him to bed."

"What?"

Waxroth gave the girl a stern look. "Diana, we are in a locked room. That tone of affronted dignity is not necessary here. For that matter, I doubt it would convince anyone if you voiced it in public."

"Werner!" Diana's cheeks were only slightly less red than her hair. Her face didn't turn red from embarrassment—Diana was not a person who got embarrassed—but from anger. She started to speak, but Waxroth cut her off.

"Diana, when I hired you, what did you think I hired you for?"

Diana put her hands on her hips. "To be your companion." She stood up. "To impress your clients. To make you look good." Her voice rose. "For eye candy, damn it! Guys in your position like to go around with beautiful women hanging all over them. They think it increases their stature. Which it probably does, considering the kind of lowlife morons you generally associate with."

"All perfectly true. And what else? When you accepted the job, didn't you think I'd expect you to sleep with me?"

Diana's pretty lips were curled around gritted teeth. "Now listen here, Werner, I don't know what kind of ..."

"I know just what kind of girl you are, Diana. That's why I hired you. I haven't had the opportunity to make use of your favors until now, but now is when you are needed."

"I am not going to seduce some teenage boy."

"You will do what I tell you to do. Because if you don't, you are going right back where I found you. It's a cruel world out there for those without money. If I recall correctly, you had only a few career options, and all of them were considerably less pleasant than sleeping with some jockey."

Diana's fists were clenching inside her opera gloves. She had to take several long, deep breaths before she thought she had her voice under control. When she was finally ready to speak, Waxroth cut her off again. "Think quickly, Diana. I'm not waiting all night. You'll do what I tell you, or you'll be plying your trade in taverns again."

"Fine," snapped Diana. "Fine! I'll do it. You can be proud of yourself, Werner. You've added pimp to your list of job skills."

"This is business. And I'm a businessman. Do a good job. Spend some money on him. If I'm guessing right, he'll be reluctant to sleep with you, so you'll need to use all of your charm."

"I know how to seduce a man, damn it!"

"Then go do it." Waxroth turned back to his writing. "Don't forget the lipstick." The gorgeous redhead whirled on her high heels and left the room, closing the door with a THUMP that shook the desk and made a blot under Waxroth's quill. He made a "tchah" noise and ran the blotter over the excess ink. A moment later Diana came back in and snatched her purse off the sideboard, even more furious that her grand exit had been ruined.

"Relax, Diana," Waxroth told her back. "Think how grateful he'll be. I will give you odds that the kid will treat you better than any of the other men you've been with."

"Go to hell, Werner," said Diana, and closed the door with another thump.

CHAPTER ELEVEN

"I've invited Doctor MacGool to dinner," Lachtenslachter told Andy. "I'm going to confess that I stole his brain."

"What!"

They were in Lachtenslachter's room. Andy was helping him dress for dinner. "It's the right thing to do, Andy. It has been weighing heavily on my conscience and, really, there is no point hiding the truth now."

"There certainly is! Finishline and Goldie need to be able to race that horse. They'll be in big trouble if they don't. You know that."

"They can't race the horse without Miss Brown."

"Sure they can. I mean, they might still find another jockey."

"I think that is highly unlikely, Andy. I don't like to give up either, so I went down to the clubhouse and asked around. I have never seen a randier group of young men in all my life. No, lad. It was, if I may say so myself, a noble experiment, but now we are forced to bring it to a conclusion."

"No, we're not." Andy tried to keep the panic out of his voice. He hadn't expected this. With the Durk's Classic less than twenty-four hours away, Doctor Lachtenslachter had decided to lay a guilt trip on himself. "Maybe Cordy can't race now, but there's still next season. Finishline and Goldie can race it in the three to five year old class. Um, of course they'll have to hide for a while—wait—maybe they can still sell it."

"Andy, that is one ill-tempered horse. They won't be able to sell it. How can they, when most trainers won't be able to ride it? They won't be able to find a buyer who can even touch it." Lachtenslachter suddenly looked thoughtful. "Of course, if they do put it up for sale, MacGool should have first chance to bid."

"But that seems a bit unfair. Doctor MacGool will be buying back his own brain."

"Hmm, yes. He should get a discount for the cost of the brain. Perhaps I should buy the horse myself. Then remove the brain and give it back to MacGool. Hmm. I suppose I need to make an offer to Finishline before he is forced to skip town." Lachtenslachter chose a collar for his shirt and fastened the studs while he spoke. "You see, Andy, a man's brain is a very personal thing. Especially for a scientist. We get very attached to our brain. I cannot tell you how many experiments have failed because the scientist did not have a brain that was adequate for the task."

"Yes, I'm starting to see how that could happen." Andy tried a different tactic. "Doctor Lachtenslachter, I see now that you're right. What I did was dishonest and dishonorable, and I should make amends. But I'm the one who stole the brain, right? I did the actual theft. In fact, I thought of it and talked everyone else into the idea. So it is only right that I should be the one to confess to Doctor MacGool. Unfortunately I have other plans for tomorrow. I ... um ... told Cordy that I would spend the day with her. So, if you'll just wait a few more days ..."

"No. No, that wouldn't be right, Andy. I can't let you take the lead on this. It will look like I'm trying to foist the blame off on my assistant. You stole the brain with my approval, so I'm ultimately responsible."

Andy tried to refrain from making a face. That was the problem with Mad Scientists. They weren't like Evil Geniuses, who just laughed maniacally when reminded of their crimes. Mad Scientists were much nicer to work with, but had a tendency to go all moral on you at the most inconvenient times. You had to sidetrack them until they got over it. "It's not only about responsibility, Doctor Lachtenslachter. It's about the truth. You said you wanted to tell Doctor MacGool the truth and the truth is that I'm the one who stole his brain."

Lachtenslachter gave him a kindly smile. "That's very noble of you, Andy. I appreciate that you are willing to cover for me. But you're wrong. This *is* about responsibility."

"Okay," said Andy, thinking as fast as he could. "You're right, you're right. But wait, we don't want to leave Finishline and Goldie without a racehorse, do we? Waxroth would break their arms or something, and then we'd be responsible. So we need to wait until another racehorse gets injured. Then we buy it before it goes to the knackers, switch the brain with the Roan Ranger, give the steppe rhinoceros brain back to Doctor MacGool, and everyone is happy. Finishline and Goldie have a horse they can race and MacGool has his rare brain back." He handed Lachtenslachter his tie.

Lachtenslachter thought this over while he was tying it. "I suppose," he said eventually. "Yes, I think you're right. That would be the best solution. The problem is that we don't know when another racehorse brain will be available. If you recall, we had to take this brain because we weren't able to get a winning racehorse brain."

"Yes, but we were pressed for time," Andy countered. "One will turn up if we wait for a while. You would not believe how many racehorses are put down each year. Cordy told me all about it. It's a brutal, dangerous sport, especially if you're a horse. They don't even have to have an accident. A lot of them go lame just from racing. I'll bet we won't have to wait long. We just have to be ready this time and get to a horse before they knock it in the head."

"Hmm. Yes, I can see possibilities there. I'll need to arrange this with Finishline, since it is his horse. Yes, all right. Keep your eyes open for a horse that goes lame."

"I'll start looking right away. In fact, I'll go to the races tomorrow."

"I appreciate that, Andy." Lachtenslachter was interrupted by a knock on the door. It was a courier with a letter. He turned it over a few times, while he spoke. "Still, I'll meet MacGool for dinner anyway, and pick up the check. I won't confess until I'm ready to return his brain, but it doesn't hurt to stay on his good side. He's not likely to be happy about it, and I certainly owe him for his trouble." Having resolved the issue for the present time, Lachtenslachter turned his attention to the letter. In the room's small desk he found a penknife, which he slid it under the sealing wax. As he unfolded the letter, a rectangle of pasteboard fell out.

Andy picked it up. "It's a ticket to the Blue Tune."

"It's from Eddie." Lachtenslachter scanned the rest of the letter. "He's inviting me to see him at tonight's show." He made no effort to hide how pleased he was. "He sent me a complimentary pass."

"Are you going?"

"Yes, yes, of course." Lachtenslachter saw Andy's expression. "No, I won't raise my voice. I won't say a word, I swear it. I'll just listen to the music and tell him that I enjoyed it."

"Good." Andy handed him the ticket. Lachtenslachter looked at it and frowned.

"Something wrong?"

"It's for the first show." Lachtenslachter went to the window, where he could see the clock in the town square. "Damn."

"You'll have to cancel dinner," said Andy. "Do you want

me to take a message to Doctor MacGool?"

"I can't cancel now. If he isn't already out the door, he's just about to leave. And this is not a good time to have him irritated at us."

Andy knew this was true, but he had a feeling he knew what was on Eddie's mind, and he didn't want to see the invitation refused. He didn't think it would be right to push Doctor Lachtenslachter into accepting it, either. Adults had to work these things out for themselves. So he merely shrugged and said nothing.

Lachtenslachter paced the room in indecision, then shoved the pasteboard ticket at Andy. "Andy, you take this ticket. Go to the first show, and tell Eddie that I am looking forward to seeing him play and I will definitely be there for the second set."

"All right!" said Andy, thinking that the evening was working out pretty well after all. He bounded back to the Horseshoe Inn to change clothes and run a wet comb through his hair. He counted his money and decided to ask Cordy if she wanted to go to the club with him. He went to her door, raised his hand to knock, thought better of it, and went back to his own room to check his look in the mirror and comb his hair again. He returned to her door, but this time he did not even try to knock. He simply walked past it to the end of the hall, turned around, and walked past it again. He went back to his own room, closed the door, sat down on the bed, and spent the next few minutes convincing himself that he hadn't lost his nerve.

Better not do it. I have to race tomorrow, and if I see her, she's going to tell me to go to bed early. Which I can't do, because I need to deliver this message from Doctor Lachtenslachter to Eddie. Of course, I could deliver the message and leave, but I've never heard Eddie play on stage. Plus, I don't even know what kind of music she likes.

He finally decided that the thing to do was wait and see how the race turned out. If things went well, he could ask Cordy out on a date to celebrate. If things didn't work out well—and he conceded to himself that they probably would not—it wouldn't be right to be out clubbing the night before their big race.

I'll ask her out after the race, he told himself. *I'll just listen to the first set, I'll give Eddie the message, and I'll come right back here and go to bed.*

He checked his look in the mirror one more time, patted

all his pockets to make sure he had everything, then left the inn, dodging between carriages and wagons on his way to the Blue Tune. It was Saturday night and the area around the town square was in full swing, with men and women, dressed in their evening finery, congregating around the doorways of the dance halls. Music and lamplight were spilling out of the tavern windows. Students from Travaillia University were standing in groups, pooling their money to buy a keg. Across the square, and a few blocks farther on, the streets became quieter and the row of streetlamps ended, but there was still enough moon and ambient light for Andy to see his way. He stopped at a corner to let a wagon rumble past. At the end of the next block he could see the blue light that marked the entrance to the Blue Tune. He had just stepped off the pavement when he felt someone brush against him.

"Oops," said a girl's voice. Andy instinctively put out an arm to steady her. She wrapped delicate hands around it. "Thank you." Her voice was a warm, rich, contralto, and her words rippled softly into his ears. "The streets are a bit muddy tonight. That's why I wore boots. Do you like them?"

Automatically Andy looked down. A long slim leg extended from a slit in her skirt. At one end was a stylish black boot, with a high spiked heel, that hugged her calf. From there Andy's eyes traveled upward, along the gentle curves of her thighs, past the amazingly narrow waist, to linger on the swells of her breasts, and the deep cleavage defined by the tight blouse. There his eyes lingered while his heart went into double-time and every gland in his body started dumping hormones into his bloodstream. It took a serious concentration of willpower to force his gaze upward until he finally looked at the girl's face, although he immediately decided the effort was well rewarded. Glossy red lipstick gleamed on the girl's soft, full lips. Long lashes set off her cool green eyes. A pair of gold hoops dangled from her ears at exactly the right height to accent her cheekbones, and the smooth, pale skin of her face was surrounded by gentle waves of fine red hair. She was heart-stoppingly beautiful. Andy knew a good deal about female anatomy from textbooks he had found in Doctor Lachtenslachter's library. He decided now the authors of those books had missed the point.

"They're very nice," he said, which wasn't exactly sparkling repartee but he thought he was doing well just to avoid babbling like an idiot. When he saw that she was steady on her feet he tried to step back, to let her walk past. To his surprise she kept her hand on his arm. She smiled at him.

"Are you going to the Blue Tune?" she asked. "It's that way."

"As a matter of fact, I am." Andy was surprised. First of all, that a girl this good-looking was making conversation with him. Andy's experience from school was that the really hot girls had "waitress eyes." They had too many guys trying to chat them up already, so they learned to look right past you without seeming to notice you. And second, he was surprised that a girl this old was talking to him at all. She had to be, he estimated, at least eighteen. The girls at school tended to ignore younger guys, even if they were athletes.

But if this babe wanted him to take her to the club, he wasn't going to argue with her. "It's the coolest club in the city," she told him as they walked. "It doesn't look like much, but it has the best music." With her high heels, her eyes were exactly level with his.

"I've heard that," Andy said. "Although I've never been there." Somehow, before he became aware of what she was doing, she had entwined her arm with his, and was leaning against him slightly as they walked. He could smell her perfume. It was not the gardenia or rose oil or apple blossom scent that other girls he knew used. It was the scent of soft skin and wet lips.

"You'll like the Blue Tune. I can tell you're a cool guy."

"Um, thanks." No girl had ever told Andy he was cool.

"There is a guitar player there who is very good," she said. "His name is Eddie Lock. He writes his own songs, too."

"I know. He's my cousin."

She looked at him with surprise. "No. Really?"

Andy thought she seemed impressed. "Oh, yes. His name is Eddie Lachtenslachter. Eddie Lock is his stage name. I used to hear him play at his father's castle all the time. This will be the first time for me to see him on stage, though."

"His father has a castle?" She looked thoughtful.

"Yeah, he got it for the lightning."

The girl looked at him strangely, as though Andy had said something weird. "There's great lightning at that location," he clarified. "I go there pretty much every summer. You know, get up in the mountains, do a little hiking, a little fishing, some grave robbing." Andy started to ask the girl her name, but then thought that might be too forward. Instead he said, "My name is An ... Andrew."

"Diana," said the girl. "And here we are." They went down the steps, under the twin blue globes that marked the entrance to the Blue Tune. Andy showed his ticket and then, after a moment's hesitation, took out his money pouch to pay for Diana. But the doorman looked at the ticket and waved them both in.

Once they were inside the club, Andy stood aside again, expecting that she would leave him to join up with her own friends. Instead she pulled him over to a small table in the back of the room. *The evening is looking better and better*, he thought. Other guys had told him about going to clubs to meet girls. Andy didn't know it was this simple. He looked around, waiting for his eyes to become accustomed to the smoke and dim light. The four-piece band was already on stage. Eddie was singing "Get Out of My Face," one of his earlier songs. A waitress appeared out of the gloom and looked at Andy expectantly. Andy wasn't sure of the procedure at this point. Obviously she expected him to pay for Diana, but should he ask Diana what she wanted, or just wait for her to order? He said, "Um, can I buy you a drink?"

"I'll tell you what," said Diana. "Why don't I buy you a drink? Bottle of the house red," she said to the waitress, who disappeared before Andy could say anything. Diana leaned over Andy. He noticed that the top two buttons of her blouse were unbuttoned, revealing a deep V of cleavage. Did that just happen now? He didn't think he could have missed seeing this before.

The sax player was doing a solo, a slow song called Mournful Morning. Eddie spotted the two of them from the stage and waved. Andy waved back.

A waiter, not the girl who took the order, showed up with a bottle and two wine glasses on a tray. He briskly uncorked the bottle and started to pour, but Diana took it out of his hand. "I'll do that. Thank you." The waiter left.

"Wait," Andy called after him, but the waiter had already gone behind the bar. "I usually just drink small beer," he told Diana.

"Oh no. You've got to help me drink this." Diana filled Andy's glass nearly to the brim. "I can't drink a whole bottle by myself." Which was often true, but only when Waxroth took it away from her. She put the bottle down and, while doing so, somehow managed to roll her shoulders so that her breasts jiggled. Andy wondered if he really needed to leave after the first set. *After all, how much sleep do I really need to ride a horse?* All the smoke in the room was making his throat dry. He picked up his glass and drank half of it down.

Andy was not normally a boy who had difficulty talking. Now he found himself wracking his brain for something to say to this girl, as every possible line of conversation made him feel like an idiot. "Do you come from around here?" he asked finally. He felt pleased with himself for thinking of an original question.

"Oh no," said Diana. "I moved here from a small town in the south. My family has a cherry orchard. When I was a little girl I had to help them pick the cherries. Of course, I couldn't resist eating some, but they'd always know because my lips would be red." She edged her chair closer to Andy and refilled his glass. "I must have looked quite a sight, Andrew. Can you just imagine me with cherry lips all wet and sticky?"

Andy had no trouble imagining this. He took back his glass and drank again. *The Durk's Classic isn't until the afternoon*, he reminded himself. *I can sleep late if I need to.*

"Sometimes the juice would drip all over my skin and I'd have to lick it off," Diana continued. "My father would get so mad if I ate too many cherries. He'd put me over his knee and spank me. Of course I knew I deserved it because I was a bad girl. But I'm still not sure it was right." She laid her hand on Andy's arm and looked into his face with troubled eyes. "What do you think, Andrew?" she asked seriously. "Even when a girl is very bad, do you think it's right to spank her smooth bare bottom?"

"Um, I really hadn't given it much thought," said Andy, although he was thinking about it now. Diana's lips were slightly open and her mouth was only inches away from his own. Her face was very clear in his eyes, but the rest of the room seemed to be receding into the distant background. The music seemed to be coming from far away, drowned out by testosterone floodwaters. He put his hand over hers. *I don't have a chance of winning anyway. It really won't matter if I don't ride tomorrow.*

At the front of the room Eddie was playing a blues classic called Melanie by Moonlight. Diana said something that Andy couldn't hear, not because the music was loud, but because she was now sitting so close her thigh was pressed against his and he couldn't concentrate on her words. He tried to remember that he was here on an errand, that he needed to tell Eddie something. He shook his head and Diana leaned even closer, so that her lips brushed against his ear. At the same time her foot twined around his ankle. That made it even harder to concentrate, even though he could feel her warm breath caressing his earlobe as she spoke.

She must have asked a question, because she drew back slightly and gave him a questioning look. Andy nodded. It was apparently the right answer, because she smiled at him in a way that made his body temperature jump three degrees on the Celsius scale. She drew his arm around her waist. Andy forgot about the Roan Ranger, the race, and everything else in the world except the beautiful girl at his side.

And the sudden silence. His ears were working fine again. It was silent because the music had stopped. He looked up to see Eddie and the band putting aside their instruments. The first set was over.

Diana rested her head on his shoulder.

Eddie liked to think he had a highly developed moral code where girls were concerned. He thought a man should be honest with a woman and always tell her the truth, as long as doing so did not interfere with getting her into bed. So he had told the green-eyed girl straight out on the first night they met, "If you want to date a musician, don't expect him to get a lot done in the mornings." Eddie had long ago decided that if you got out of bed before noon, you were really missing out on the main advantage of the musician lifestyle. Apparently the green-eyed girl agreed with him, because when he finally did wake up—and on this day it wasn't until nearly two o'clock—she was still asleep, pressed up against him with one slender arm thrown over his chest.

He lay awake and reflected on the previous evening. His father had arrived late, but that was okay since he had sent Andy to say he was going to be late. They hadn't talked much, but they hadn't argued either, so that was okay too. Eddie had played a jazzed up version of the pizzicato polka, which his father seemed to like and the rest of the crowd didn't mind too much. (He made it the first song of the third set, when the customers were still getting their drinks refilled and not paying much attention to the band.) Then the club had closed up and, as usual, he hung around to jam for a few hours with the other musicians. The green-eyed girl stayed on to go to breakfast with them, and she had followed him back to his rooms.

His thoughts were interrupted by a kiss. The girl in question had woken up. He pushed her red hair out of his face, kissed her back, and let her snuggle into the crook of his arm. "Hey Diana," he said, "don't you have to get back to your boss?" Immediately he felt the slim body grow tense. "Hey, it's okay."

Diana kept her eyes closed for a few minutes before she opened them and answered. "I'm not going back."

Eddie said, "Oh?"

"Don't worry, Eddie. I'm not forcing myself on you. I'll find a place to stay."

"Ah, okay." Eddie tried not to sound relieved. "Of course, you can stay with me until you find a place."

"You don't really mean that."

"Sure I do," said Eddie, and was surprised to find that he did.

Diana hesitated again before she spoke. She ran one finger over his chest, tracing the scars. "Well, maybe just tonight."

"Tonight is fine. So what happened? I thought you had a good position with Waxroth. Just what you wanted. Nice clothes, nice restaurants, nice apartment with a great view. You get to meet interesting people and watch him threaten them."

"It's hard to explain. He just went too far. It was one thing to treat me like his mistress, even though I wasn't. I thought he was just keeping me around for decoration. And yes, okay, I admit I would have become his mistress, if it came to that. But then he decided to treat me like a prostitute."

Eddie frowned. "He wanted to pay you for sleeping with him?"

"No," said Diana. "He wanted me to sleep with other men."

"Ah. Yeah, I can see where that would be going too far."

"I mean, there's a thin line between being a mistress and being a prostitute. I know that maybe men don't see the difference, but there is. And I almost crossed it last night. I almost did what he wanted me to do."

"But you didn't. So don't worry about it."

"The decision was taken out of my hands. The kid I was supposed to seduce left after the first set. I must be losing my touch."

"Oh yeah?" Eddie placed a hand on Diana's thigh. He ran it over the curve of her hips, across her flat stomach, and let it rest under the swell of her breast. "You must have found it again pretty quickly." He gave her a long kiss, then raised his head to look around for his shirt. He saw it hanging on the back of a chair, disentangled himself from Diana, and rolled out of bed. "I guess that guy came and left while I was on stage. I only saw you with Andy."

"Yes, he said he was your cousin."

"Andy?"

"Right." Diana propped her head on one elbow and looked at Eddie. A lock of red hair covered one green eye. "Why are you smiling?"

"Andy? Come on, Diana. He's still in school. You're telling me that your boss, Werner Waxroth, ordered you to sleep with Andy?" Eddie buttoned his shirt. "I'm sorry, baby, but I think you either made a mistake, or Andy must be having a lot more interesting summers than he ever had when I was around."

Diana sat up and stretched, which lifted her breasts in a way that made Eddie stop buttoning his shirt until she lowered her arms. He looked out the window and wondered if there was time to go back to bed. He couldn't see the sun, but the shadows on the windowsill told him it was getting late into the afternoon.

She said, "I didn't make a mistake. Werner wrote down his name and gave me a description. He knew all about him. He even knew that he was staying at the Horseshoe Inn. Now you're laughing at me."

"I'm not laughing at you, baby. I'm just laughing. I had no idea Waxroth and Andy were such good friends."

"They're not friends. Andy didn't know Werner put me up to it. I was supposed to seduce him. I told you." Diana shrugged, letting the sheets slip further down her slim body, until they pooled around her waist. "You know, I didn't expect him to put up so much resistance. Usually with a teenage boy, all you have to do is throw him a sultry look and he'll do anything."

"Really?" Eddie said. "I'm surprised that you would say that. You mean it takes more than a sultry look *after* we're teens?"

"Maybe my sultry looks are fading."

Eddie leaned over the bed to kiss her again. "I think your sultry look is plenty sultry enough." She arched her back for the kiss, pushing her breasts toward him. When he finished he said, "So what is the whole story? Is your boss so tired of bookmaking and loan–sharking that he wants to branch out into grave–robbing? Does he need to have a clavicle replaced and doesn't want to pay full retail? Or is this just his way of encouraging promising young science students?"

"I don't know." Diana got out of bed and wrapped the sheet around her, in a demure manner that was actually calculated to be enticing. She pretended to look for her clothes. "Werner somehow got the idea that if your cousin had sex last night, he wouldn't be able to ride in today's race. It's one of those sports myths. You know, a lot of athletes abstain from sex the night before a game. They think it will weaken them. But not being able to ride a horse at all? Werner has a lot of money at risk in the Durk's Classic. I think it's making him a bit mad."

"Well, for a gambler like Waxroth, you can't find a safer bet than that. Andy won't ride a horse in any race. Hey, if I promise not to race horses, will Waxroth assign you to sleep with me? That would certainly make dating easier. Cuts out all that 'are you free this Saturday?' stuff."

Diana bent over at the waist, with her legs straight and her pert round bottom in the air. When she stood up she was holding a tiny scrap of lace that might have been underwear. "Have you seen my stockings? Your cousin is riding in the Durk's Classic. I checked the scratch sheet. You should go there and root for him. I thought he was nice. You still have time to get there."

Eddie stood very still. "Andy is riding in a horse race?"

"The Durk's Classic. He's listed as an amateur jockey. Hey, let's both go to the race. You and me. It will be fun. Have you ever been to the Durk's Classic? It's a madhouse. A giant drunken party, with horses. We can cheer for your cousin."

"Impossible." Eddie pulled on his pants and started looking for his shoes. "I'd better check, anyway. What inn did you say he was staying at?"

"The Horseshoe Inn. A lot of jockeys and racetrack people stay there. It's on the way to the track. Eddie, is something wrong?"

"No," said Eddie, buttoning his shoes at top speed. "No, not really. I'm going over there." His big fingers yanked a button off one shoe. "Damn." Without bothering to finish the other shoe he pushed the door open. Diana made a hasty grab at the sheets to cover herself.

"Diana, I'm going out for a bit. This shouldn't take long. Then I'll come back and we'll go eat something, okay? See you later."

Mystified, Diana ran to the window and watched him walk down the street in the direction of the track. Eddie started by walking fast, then walked faster, then broke into a run. He disappeared around a corner.

She decided to follow him.

Eddie reached the Horseshoe Inn and found the proprietor studying a racing form. "I'm looking for my cousin Andy, younger than me, about so high, kind of skinny, fair hair. Is he staying here?"

"I know him." The proprietor held up his racing form and pointed to Andy's name. "The new amateur jockey, right? He's staying here, but of course he's at the races now. Everyone who stays here goes to the races. I'd be there myself if I didn't have to mind the business. Today is the Durk's Classic."

"It's got to be a mistake. He's not at the Durk's Classic. He can't be. What room is he in?"

The proprietor looked at Eddie quickly, and decided that when a muscular young man with a wicked collection of scars asked him for information, he was not going to reply with a lecture on privacy. He reached for the register. Eddie took it out of his hands, flipped the page, saw Andy's signature, and took the stairs two at a time. Andy's door was locked. He pounded on it, forced himself to wait for an answer, then pounded on it again. He even considered forcing it open, but realized that was stupid. Andy wasn't inside.

Nothing to worry about, he told himself. *He doesn't sleep late like you. He's out and about. There's lots of stuff he could be doing. He wouldn't be stupid enough to ride in a horse race.*

He went back down the stairs at double time and out the door of the inn, where he ran into Diana and nearly knocked her over. She grabbed his arms. "Eddie, what's wrong?"

"Where's the racetrack?"

"This way."

Eddie broke into a run.

"Eddie!"

"His back!" Eddie shouted over his shoulder. "Andy has a bad back! If he's thrown, it could paralyze him for life!"

Diana ran after him.

CHAPTER TWELVE

"They've got the rollers out," said Cordy with satisfaction. "They're expecting rain."

"Is that good?" said Andy.

"It's good if it doesn't rain. They roll the track to press the dirt down so the rain doesn't wash it away. That means a smooth track and a fast race." She pointed to the Roan Ranger. "It will be easier to control him on a smooth track."

"Uh huh."

"He's good on a fast track."

"Uh huh."

"And the track will be nice and hard."

"A hard track. Oh, great."

They were in the dressing room. The other jockeys had already dressed and weighed in. Andy strapped on his breast pad, and then pulled the silk jersey over it. It had a large checkerboard pattern of green and gold squares, the colors of the stable where Finishline rented training equipment. Cordy looked at Andy critically. "You're a little overweight."

"I certainly am not! What are you talking about? I'm totally ripped. I'm buff. I'm height weight proportional!"

"Overweight for a jockey, I mean. Too much muscle is as bad as too much fat. Here." Cordy unwrapped a parcel. "I borrowed these for you. These are extra thin riding boots. They're what we wear when we're trying to stay below weight."

She held up a pair of tan riding boots. Andy took them from her. Normal racing boots were already pretty light. He felt like he was wearing kid leather gloves on his feet. But these had been shaved to an extreme thinness—it seemed to him that they were little more than parchment with boot polish. He put them on anyway and was about to comment on them when he saw the saddle.

"That's a saddle?"

"A racing saddle. Very light weight."

"I'll say. There's nothing to it. It's not like the one we trained with."

"Don't worry, it works the same way. You were using an exercise saddle. Exercise saddles have more support, because when a horse is being exercised he might try to throw the rider."

"Oh, and he won't try to throw me during the race?"

"Of course not. He'll be too busy running."

"Right. Obviously."

"Unless he throws you before the race. Once you get him into the gate he'll be fine."

"Uh huh."

Cordy's next step was to produce a bridle with a ring bit. Even Andy knew what *that* was for. It was for horses that were hard to control.

She saw him looking at it. "Don't worry about it."

"I'm not worried." Andy took the bridle from Cordy and went into the weighing room. He sat on the weighing chair with all his equipment gathered on his lap. Weights were solemnly added to the other side of the scale until it balanced. The Clerk of the Scale didn't tell him he had to carry more weight so apparently Cordy was right.

He went out the other side of the weighing room, shifted all the equipment to one arm, and unlatched the door to the Roan Ranger's stall. Typically there was one groom for every four horses, but Andy and Cordy had been caring for the Roan Ranger themselves, as the horse was always antagonistic to anyone who did not meet its high standards of chastity. Andy was sure he'd never be riding it through Travaillia's red light district.

A moment later he wasn't sure he'd be riding it anywhere at all. A steel-shod hoof hit the stall door with an angry kick. Andy fell back. "Hey!" he said out loud. "It's me!"

The answer was a loud snort. Andy peeked into the stall. The Roan Ranger was in the far corner, glaring at him with undisguised hostility. It pawed viciously at the ground, ready for a fight.

"Hey! What are you upset about?"

The horse gave him a don't-try-to-pretend-to-me look.

"What? That girl at the club last night? The redhead? I never even kissed her, I swear it!"

The horse responded with a snort of disbelief.

"It's true. There was never anything between us. It was just a casual fling. She means nothing to me."

The Roan Ranger looked mollified, but still suspicious.

"Sure, I looked," Andy conceded. "A guy can look, can't he? But nothing happened. Maybe I was tempted, but it was just a moment of weakness." The Roan Ranger picked up a mouthful of hay and chewed it thoughtfully. Andy approached closer. "Just give me one more chance. Think of all we've been through together. Are you going to throw all that away? I can change, I promise."

Cordy came into the stall. "Andy, what are you doing?"

"Nothing. Just checking." Andy slipped the bridle onto the Roan Ranger and whispered in its ear, "So you and me, we're still a team, right? Come on, we've got a race to run." The horse glared at him from one eye. "Don't look at me that way. Wait until some hot unicorn babe offers to buy *you* a shot of alfalfa. I'll bet you'll change your tune."

"Let's go."

"We're coming." He followed Cordy to the saddling paddock. The other horses, jockeys, and trainers were already at work. At Geht Downs, the horses were saddled in the open, so the betting public could watch and be assured there was no skullduggery involved. Normally few people came to watch, but today was the Durk's Classic and the crowd was three deep around the rails, looking over the horses and riders before placing their bets. Most people were interested only in the favorites, Jumping Jack Flask and Armadillo. The Roan Ranger snorted and glared at the spectators, but kept his temper. As best she could with one arm still in a sling, Cordy helped Andy strap on the saddle and fix blinders to the bridle.

"We have to walk him around the paddock so the fans can see he's saddled properly. Then I'll boost you into the saddle."

Andy gave her a look. "Thank you, Cordy, but I can get on a horse by myself."

"I know, I know, but it's a tradition. Now from this point on, you can't talk to anyone in the crowd, or touch anyone except by accident, or take anything from anyone except myself or the owner. Oh, and this is important. You must stay on the horse after you win the race. If you dismount before you enter the Winner's Circle, you'll be disqualified."

"Huh. I didn't know that. Winner's Circle, right." He patted the Roan Ranger on the neck. "Don't throw me until we're in the Winner's Circle. Got it?"

Andy placed a foot in the stirrup. Cordy made a pretense of pushing him up with her good arm, for tradition's sake, after which he swung himself onto the Roan Ranger. It accepted this calmly enough, although Cordy grabbed the bridle and kept a solid grip on it until Andy was firmly seated and they were both sure he had the Roan Ranger under control. They had learned that although the Roan Ranger had a unicorn's affection for virgins, it also had its own mind. It needed a hard hand on the reins to keep it in line.

Finishline and Goldie were waiting when they came out of the saddling paddock. They stayed well away, so as not to anger the horse, but it still became skittish at their presence. Andy guided the horse on the dirt path to the track. Finishline called Cordy over. "Do we have a plan?"

"Our plan is to get out in front and stay there. It's his first race, so we won't try anything tricky. He'll get in trouble if he tries to get through the pack."

"Does Andy know that?"

"Of course. We went all through it. I'll see you at the Winner's Circle."

"Okay."

Goldie waved to Andy, who waved back. "Cordy, tell Andy good luck for us."

"I will."

Cordy ran to follow Andy, who had taken the rear of the procession of horses that were on their way to the track. Finishline and Goldie walked past the grandstand. It was completely full today. The Durk's Classic was the highlight of the racing season, attracting race fans and horse breeders from throughout the continent. Scattered through the crowd were the attractive spokesmodels that the Durk's brewery hired to promote beer. Behind the grandstand was the clubhouse, and at the top of the stands were the private boxes containing the best views and the most expensive seats. Goldie came abreast of Waxroth's box just as he entered it. The bookmaker looked down but didn't notice them.

"He hangs up there like a vulture on a cliff," she said. "Staring down, waiting for a chance to prey on the weak. Even though he doesn't look particularly vulpine himself."

"Vulpine means like a fox, sweetie."

"Vulturous? Vulturine?"

"One of those."

One after another, the jockeys guided their mounts out of the brick and grass paddock, along a short, sawdust-lined road, through a white wooden gate, and onto the track, where they paraded past the stands on the way to the starting gate. Alongside the stands were the tote boards, where the on-track bookmakers took bets and marked up the odds. Cordy winced a little when she saw the boards. The odds against the Roan Ranger, which everyone knew had been injured in its last race, had started out high. The odds had come down when the betting public learned that National Cordy, a celebrity jockey, had been hired to ride it. Now that the touts knew an amateur jockey would be taking her place, the odds against Andy and the Roan Ranger skyrocketed.

Andy halted the Roan Ranger to watch three carts cross the track into the midway. There was a white cart, the ambulance, pulled by a white carthorse and driven by two white-suited men. There was a big black cart, the horse ambulance, pulled by two strong draft horses. And following the two ambulances was a high black wagon, the knacker's cart. It was draped with black crepe cloth to cover the words "Farlong Hides and Pet Food." He turned his head away from this and looked for Cordy. She was standing at the rail. She waved to him. He waved back.

They had drawn the third position in the starting gate. The Roan Ranger entered it without a problem. Andy guessed he was eager to run, and that overcame his dislike for the other riders. Cordy thought that number three in the gate was a good position. She didn't want to see him start too close in, where he might get squeezed against the rail.

An elderly couple recognized her and asked for her autograph. She smiled, signed their program books quickly, then sought out Finishline and Goldie. They were in back of the stands, running their eyes over the tote boards. "Is the fix in?" she asked them. "Who is it?"

"I am not at all certain I can guess," said Finishline. "We are looking for a sudden change in the odds, which indicates that someone is placing large, last minute bets. However I do not see any such change. The bookmakers tell me that most people are still betting the chalk." By this he meant they were betting on the favorites.

"Waxroth is too clever for that," said Goldie. "I'm sure he told his people to place lots of little bets, and spread them out over time."

"But," said Cordy, "he wants a horse that has long odds against it. He fixed this race so he can bet on his own horse and make more money." She looked toward the box seats. Waxroth had been joined by one of his henchmen.

"That is not necessarily true," said Finishline. "Remember he is not only placing bets, he is taking bets. He might offer good odds against a horse that is favored to win, so lots of people will bet on it. Then he fixes the race so that horse loses. Armadillo, I am thinking. He is good on a dirt track. In his three previous races he is first, first, and second at the post."

"But he's carrying more weight this time," said Goldie. "My guess is Dental Carrie. She has a good bloodline, out of Carrie Granite and Wisdom Tooth, and she is a strong finisher."

"My choice would be Thatzafact," said Cordy. "I rode her twice. She's an excellent horse, fast and good out of the gate. But the Roan Ranger is better." She turned to the rail.

"They are all excellent horses in the Durk's Classic," said Finishline glumly. "And excellent jockeys."

"You have a fast horse," Cordy called over her shoulder. "Don't worry." She elbowed her way back to the rail. On the other side of the track the caller mounted his platform. He wiped the mouthpiece of his bullhorn and bellowed into it.

"It's a beautiful day for a race. Number one is Armadillo, number two is Jumping Jack Flask, number three is Roan Ranger, number four is Stitchin Time, number five is Dental Carrie, number six is Savannah, Off The Record has been scratched, and number eight is Thatzafact." He spoke over the applause for Armadillo. As he paused for breath there was a round of applause for Thatzafact.

Cordy felt Finishline and Goldie come up behind her. She turned around and looked at their faces. They were grave, both silent, too nervous even to applaud their own horse. At the tote boards the bookmakers stopped taking bets. She turned to the track. She could only see Andy's back, as he sat hunched over the Roan Ranger's neck. The caller raised his bullhorn again. "The horses are in the starting gate." The starter raised his hammer and took aim at the bell.

Cordy heard a commotion behind her.

Turple and Mukkleson had spent their lives around horses. At an early age they had been apprenticed to muck out stalls and clean stables, and from those humble beginnings had graduated to successful careers in mucking stalls and cleaning stables. Eventually they had gotten too old and too arthritic for heavy cleaning work. Now they stood at the entrance to Geht Downs, one at each side of the gate. They were given the posts as sort of retirement positions. They took tickets, answered questions, gave directions, and were generally pretty good about stopping little boys and impoverished gamblers from trying to sneak in. But there's a limit to what you can ask a couple of old men to do. When a muscular young man ran through the gate without stopping, they each noted the scars running down his sinewy arms, exchanged glances with each other, and decided to look the other way.

Less than a minute later a beautiful young woman, her long red hair streaming behind her, ran through the gate. She was clad in only a sheet. This time Turple and Mukkleson did not look the other way. But they still let her through.

Eddie stopped in the middle of the concourse, realizing that he didn't know where to go. Around him he could see only people and the grandstand. He pushed through the crowd until he saw a long, low building. He guessed it was the stable and ran towards it. In fact, it was the clubhouse. He reached it just as Lachtenslachter came out, holding a sausage in a bun and a mug of Durk's beer. He saw Eddie and waved. "Eddie! What a pleasant surprise."

"Dad!" Eddie stopped beside Lachtenslachter, trying to catch his breath.

Lachtenslachter looked at him quizzically. "I didn't know you liked horse racing, Eddie. Do you know they give guided tours of the stables here? I must bring Deedee one of these days. She'd get a kick out of it. She loves horses."

"It's Andy," Eddie said between pants. "He's going to ride a racehorse."

Lachtenslachter looked around in alarm. "He wouldn't do that."

"Why not?" asked Diana, catching up with them. "Why wouldn't he ride a racehorse?"

"His back," Eddie repeated. "Andy was a hunchback. Dad operated on him to straighten it."

"I did the best I could," said Lachtenslachter, "but it's not very strong."

"Andy's been doing these special exercises. But if he twists his back, or jars it ..."

"If a horse were to throw him ..."

"The stables are that way," said Diana, pointing. "And the saddling paddock is that way."

"I'll take the stables," said Eddie, and disappeared in the crowd.

"The paddock," said Lachtenslachter and ran in that direction. Diana started to follow him, but she was stopped by a meaty hand that clamped down over her shoulder. The hand turned her around until she was staring into a face that looked like it had been assembled from broken parts.

"Hello, Diana," said Grogan. "The Boss wants to see you."

The cheetah is the fastest land animal. It can reach speeds of up to seventy miles an hour. It can accelerate from zero to seventy in three seconds. The cheetah is a mighty fast cat, but it travels on its own. You can't ride a cheetah.

You can't ride a greyhound either, although it may reach forty-five miles an hour. It's possible to ride an elephant, but it will only carry you at a fast walk. On the other hand, that walk can reach twenty-four miles per hour. Still, very few people get the opportunity to race an elephant.

It's far easier, and much less expensive, to get your hands on a saddle mule. A really good saddle mule, with its rider, might hit thirty-five miles an hour. Thirty-five miles an hour is pretty fast. You don't want to hit the ground at thirty-five miles an hour.

And then there's the race horse.

Andy risked a quick glance to either side. The other jockeys were staring straight ahead, knees bent up to their waists, hands tightly curled around the reins, their whips pointed either straight up or straight back. There was no talking, no making of those encouraging noises to the horse that goes on in the paddock. They were grim and silent, waiting for the starting bell, totally focused on the track in front of them and the race ahead of them.

He felt the Roan Ranger's flanks swelling and falling with each breath. He put a palm against the horse's neck and felt the quivering of taut sinew. He was on an animal that, in a few short seconds, was going to accelerate to more than fifty miles per hour, and the only thing keeping Andy on its back were a few thin pieces of leather.

There was nothing else in Travaillia that could reach fifty miles an hour. There was nothing in the world that could carry a rider at fifty miles per hour. When the starting gate dropped Andy was going to become, quite literally, one of the fastest men alive.

The bell rang.

CHAPTER THIRTEEN

Lachtenslachter was not familiar with racing, but when he found the saddling paddock was both empty and bereft of spectators, he quickly figured out that Andy had already been through it. He ran toward the track, stopping when the press of bodies impeded his way. He stood on his toes, peering over the crowd, until he noticed a bouffant of brass-blond hair. "Mrs. Theis!" he shouted.

Goldie turned around. She bobbed up and down until she saw him, and waved at him cheerfully.

"Where is Andy?" Lachtenslachter shouted back.

"Over here," he thought he heard Goldie say. A feeling of relief washed through him. Andy wasn't riding. He was just watching with his friends. He worked his way through the crowed, smiling and nodding and saying "Excuse me." Most of the people he edged past were in a good mood and let him through. When he got closer he saw Finishline's battered hat and Cordy's cap. His professional instincts made him check to see if she was carrying her broken arm properly. Goldie said something to Finishline, who turned, saw Lachtenslachter, and held out his hand.

"Hello, Doctor. I am glad you are here to join us. We are no little excited at this point, as you undoubtedly expect."

"Yes, certainly, good luck," said Lachtenslachter, looking around. "Where is Andy?"

"Right there," said Cordy, pointing. "Gate three. Colors are green and gold."

Lachtenslachter felt his stomach tighten. He could see the jockeys' backs as they hunched forward in their saddles, their faces close to the manes of their mounts. "Andy!" he yelled. His words were lost in the sudden clang of a bell, and a high, feverish roar of excitement from the crowd around him.

"They're off!" bellowed the caller.

Above the grandstands at Geht Downs were the small private boxes, big enough for two people. Above those was a row of the large private boxes, which held four people. Waxroth had one of the luxury boxes at the very top of the stands, big enough to hold a table with service for six, a box where you could give a luncheon for your friends while watching the races. As apparently he had done earlier today, for plates holding the remains of tea sandwiches and fruit salad remained on the table. Many times Diana had sat at his side, sipping sparkling wine and smiling while Waxroth buffed his connections with the local movers and shakers. He had antique chairs at the front of the box, and a polished brass spyglass balanced on a tripod for a close-up view. Waxroth was looking through the spyglass when Grogan dragged Diana to the door and roughly shoved her into the box. Below she could hear the caller bellowing into his megaphone. "Roan Ranger takes an early lead. Dental Carrie has trouble getting out of the gate. Armadillo in second place with Savannah on his tail, followed by Jumping Jack Flask, Stitchin Time, and Thatzafact."

"Diana," said Waxroth, without looking up from his spyglass. "What is that kid doing on that horse? I told you to go to bed with him."

"How do you know I didn't, Werner? And why do you care, anyway?"

"I know because ..." Waxroth looked up to see Grogan's mystified expression. He changed the subject, his glance taking in Diana's tousled hair and the bed sheet clinging to her slim figure. "You sure as hell slept with someone and I won't have you freelancing on me.

"Coming into the backstretch," came the faint voice of the caller. "It's the Roan Ranger by four lengths. Jumping Jack Flask and Savannah are neck and neck, Armadillo is half a length behind, followed by Stitchin Time, Thatzafact, and Dental Carrie bringing up the rear."

"You don't own me, Werner. I'll sleep with whom I please."

"He's pulling away," shouted Cordy, letting all her excitement show. She jumped up and down. "Yes! This is awesome. That is one fast horse. I've never seen anything like him. He's going to break the track record."

"It is not over until it is over," cautioned Finishline. But he was smiling. Beside him, Goldie started humming 'We're in the Money.'

"I just want him to finish," said Lachtenslachter. "Damn it. What possessed Andy to ride in the Durk's Classic?"

"There's nothing to worry about now," said Cordy. "All he has to do is stay on."

"Going into the far turn," said the caller. "Roan Ranger is pulling away. Jumping Jack Flask is dropping back. Savannah leads Armadillo by a head, followed by Stitchin Time, Thatzafact, and trailing the pack is Dental Carrie."

"God damn it!" Waxroth scowled at the track. The crowd grew more and more exited. The noise level below them increased. "I have a lot of money invested in this race, Diana. *A lot of money*, and if that horse wins I'm going to take it out of your ass."

"Yeah, Werner?" Diana stepped to the front of the box and leaned over. "Go Roan Ranger!" she screamed.

Without turning his head Waxroth struck her a backhand blow. The slap sent her reeling away from the rail. She staggered and fell. "Get her out of here."

Grogan grabbed a handful of Diana's hair and hauled her roughly to her feet. Her nose was bleeding. "Let's go."

"Excuse me."

Grogan looked up. A tall young man with scarred arms was standing in the entrance to the box. "Is there some trouble here?"

"Coming out of the far turn." The caller was talking fast now, and louder, to keep above the crowd noise. "Roan Ranger, Savannah, Armadillo. Jumping Jack Flask in fourth place, followed by Stitchin Time, Thatzafact, and Dental Carrie."

Finishline and Goldie were hugging each other. Lachtenslachter was smiling with relief. Inwardly he congratulated himself for putting a row of double stitches into the Roan Ranger's thighs. Andy was coming into the stretch, and since he led the whole way, his silks were still gleaming gold and green. The other horses were brown with tossed up dust and dirt. Lachtenslachter decided that he would hire an artist to paint this moment. He patted Cordy on the shoulder.

She frowned and leaned over the rail.

"No trouble, kid," Grogan said, maintaining his grip on Diana, while he flexed the fingers of his free hand. "No trouble, unless you stick around. This is a private box."

"I was just leaving," Eddie assured him. "But I'll take Diana with me." He stepped forward.

"I don't think so, kid. Mr. Waxroth has plans for her." Grogan stepped forward also. The two men were now within an arm's length of each other.

Waxroth was intent on watching the race. He looked up once, just to give a quick glance at Eddie, to snap at Diana, "So that's the boyfriend, eh?" and to tell Grogan, "Hurt him." Then he turned back to his telescope. He was unconcerned. He had Grogan to deal with issues like this.

Diana was concerned. She looked from one man to the other. They were eyeing each other, sizing each other up. Eddie had his knees flexed. He was holding his hands up with the palms out, in what Diana recognized as some sort of weird martial arts position. Grogan had one big hand clenched into a big, big fist. Eddie was tall and well-muscled, but Grogan still had a few inches in height on him and was bulkier. Eddie was younger and maybe faster, but Grogan had experience. He beat people up all the time. That was his job.

And now he moved. For such a big man he was very fast. He threw Diana down and at the same time threw a punch at Eddie, a fast punch, straight from the shoulder, and powerful enough to stun an ox.

But fast as he was, Eddie was faster. He caught Grogan's fist in both hands. Even before Grogan could bring his other fist into play, Eddie spun, twisted Grogan's arm, and quite neatly popped the big man's shoulder out of its socket.

A dislocated shoulder is not the most painful injury that a man can suffer. Most sports doctors agree that a dislocated knee is the most painful, and a majority will tell you that a dislocated hip is more painful than any shoulder injury. Still, a dislocated shoulder ranks right up there in the top five.

It dropped Grogan to his knees. He landed with a thunk on the hardwood floor of the box and stayed there, his head bent down, one arm across his chest, the other arm still being twisted by Eddie. His mouth opened but no words came out, just a long, drawn out, "Gaaaaaaaaaaah!"

Eddie heard a slight scrape of metal. Waxroth had yanked the telescope out of the tripod and was holding it like a club. Eddie dropped Grogan's arm, causing another hiss of pain. "Time to go," he said, and quickly pulled Diana to her feet. She came willingly enough, but not without a final word.

"Oh, does that hurt, Grogan?" She poked him in the shoulder as Eddie dragged her past.

"Gah!"

"Oh, too bad. But at least it's not broken."

"Get out!" Waxroth said.

"Coming down the home stretch. Roan Ranger out in front." The caller had both hands wrapped around his bullhorn, playing it across the crowd like a spotlight. In the stands the crowd was on its feet, but the cheering was subdued, except for the ecstatic cries of those few desperate gamblers who had bet on the long shot. The rest were waiting to see who came in second. "Armadillo, Jumping Jack Flask, Savannah." Lachtenslachter closed his eyes with relief. Tears of joy were welling up in Goldie's eyes. Cordy squinted down the track and said again. "Something's wrong. He's out of control."

"Jumping Jack Flask, Armadillo, Savannah, Stichin Time, Thatzafact, and Dental Carrie."

Once she said it, Finishline recognized it too. It was subtle, but Roan Ranger was no longer a fast horse under the control of a jockey, he was runaway horse, out of his mind and completely oblivious to the bit in his mouth or Andy's desperate handling of the reins. He was still at a full gallop, but he was drifting across the track while Armadillo closed the gap between them. Finishline grabbed Cordy's arm. "Get away from the rail," he shouted. "He's coming to you!"

Cordy tried to push herself away, but the press of the crowd behind her kept firmly against the rail. Finishline tapped her shoulders. Cordy understood and dropped to her knees. Finishline, Goldie, and Lachtenslachter huddled over her, trying to shield her from the sight of the crazed beast now angling directly toward them.

It didn't work. The Roan Ranger crossed the track and with a leap that would have done credit to a show jumper, cleared the inner rail, the outer rail, and sailed directly over their heads. The crowd's excited cheering turned to screams. Cordy flattened herself on the ground, with Finishline and Goldie beside her. Lachtenslachter stood in dumbstruck horror as a half-ton of horse went by his head. The spectators around him, once densely packed, now scattered, miraculously clearing a circle where the Roan Ranger came down. Its knees buckled and it almost stumbled, but it kept its balance. Then, as soon as its rear hooves touched the ground, it kicked them back up, sending its hindquarters in the air and Andy over its head.

Even before Andy hit the ground Lachtenslachter was in motion, shoving people out of his way. Andy turned a somersault and hit the ground with a sickening CRACK. His racing helmet bounced away. He lay still, his eyes closed. A moment later Lachtenslachter knelt beside him. Automatically he groped for a pulse. At the same he felt, rather than saw, other people close in around him. He lifted one of Andy's eyelids and inspected the pupil for dilation. "Don't move him," he said to the person beside him.

It was Cordy. She burst into tears. "Is he ... is he hurt?"

Andy's eyes popped open. "Well, of course I'm *hurt*," he snapped. "Everything *hurts*. But I'm not dead. Jeez, get away from me, will you?"

"And the winner is Dental Carrie," said the caller, quite calmly.

"Don't try to move," Lachtenslachter said sternly. "You could have a spinal injury and any movement at this point—oh, for goodness sake," he finished as Andy rolled over on his side. "Leave you paralyzed. Is anything broken?"

"Here, kid. Let me give you a hand up." Finishline took Andy's shoulder and steadied him. Andy stood up shakily. "How do you feel?"

"Awful," Andy told them. Cordy threw her arms around him and kissed him. "A lot better, now."

"Can you wiggle your toes?" she asked. She studied his feet.

"What? Why?"

"I don't know. That's what people always ask me when I take a fall."

"I'm not the toe–wiggling type." Andy looked around the circle of concerned faces. "Where's our horse?"

Finishline pointed. "There."

The Roan Ranger was easy to find. They just looked in the direction of screaming. The horse had run up into the grandstand. Women, children, and men with common sense were clearing away from it. A dozen or so heroic types were trying to show how brave they were by circling around it and trying to grab its bridle. But the horse was rearing and kicking like a wild bronco exposed to the dangerous end of a rattlesnake, and its flashing hooves were keeping potential captors at bay. Then it spotted Waxroth.

He was still in his private box at the top of the stands, watching the end of the race with a grim expression, watching Dental Carrie being led out of the Winner's Circle, watching Jumping Jack Flask being led in, watching a young, pretty spokesmodel hand a bottle of Durk's beer to the jockey. Waxroth ignored Grogan, who was still in the back of the box, clutching his arm. And he paid no attention to the Roan Ranger after it left the race.

Until it came straight at him.

It charged across the top of the benches. Brightly painted wood cracked and splintered beneath steel-shod hooves driven by a thousand pounds of muscle. Waxroth dropped his telescope and stared. The horse picked up speed, its head held low and pointed directly at the financier. Drops of sweat rained from its coat. It was blowing foam, and fire was in its eyes. When it reached the top of the stands it jumped.

Waxroth broke out of his trance. He stepped backward and turned to run, but the edge of a chair caught him behind the knees, and he fell back into it. The horse cleared the railing and landed in the box, right in front of Waxroth. It lowered its head until its eyes were level with the big man sitting in the chair. It stared at him. Waxroth stared back. The entire racetrack became quiet. The reputation of the Roan Ranger had spread. Most of the people there had heard that it was a mean horse. And everyone at the track recognized Werner Waxroth. Now they watched the big mean horse confront the big mean man.

At which point the horse lowered itself to its knees and laid its head in Waxroth's lap.

Waxroth looked at the horse. He looked around. Ten thousand people were staring at him, mystified. He looked for Grogan, who had propped himself on a chair and was also staring at him, equally mystified. He looked at the horse again. He snarled, "Get this thing away from me."

CHAPTER FOURTEEN

"That two-timing beast!" said Andy. "And after all we meant to each other! How could he do this to me? Why, I was saving myself for that horse. And he threw me over for another man. I gave him the best years of my life. Or at least the best days of my summer. Except for the summer days that are still to come, of course."

"I still can't understand boys," said Cordy, "Why do you all hate to admit that you've never done it?"

"It's just a guy thing, I guess," said Andy. "One of those—what do you call it—rites of passage? Rites of adulthood?"

"Coming of age ritual?"

"Yeah, something like that. Stuff that separates the men from the boys."

They were back in Barrenstock, up on the ramparts of the Castle Lachtenslachter. It was a bright, clear day, with the combination of hot sun and cool mountain air making perfect summer weather. Birds cheeped drowsily in the trees, and the occasional bumblebee braved the heights long enough to give them an inquisitive buzz before losing interest and descending again. From the walls they could look down the wildflower-covered slopes all the way to the village. Along the road the grocer's boy was approaching, carrying a hamper with the day's delivery.

"Well, no one can doubt that Waxroth is a grown man," said Cordy, picking up the thread again. "And he's still embarrassed."

"Maybe he doubts himself."

"It must really bother him, considering how much money he paid."

If Finishline and Goldie had anything in common, it was that they both knew how to seize an opportunity. While Cordy and Andy subdued the Roan Ranger, Finishline and Goldie helped Waxroth extricate himself from his box, then accompanied him back to his office. Two hours later they emerged with their debts settled and a bag of money in hand. Ownership of the Roan Ranger had been transferred to the financier. Waxroth later appeared and told onlookers that horses always liked him. "Dogs, too. I'm just one of those people who has a way with animals." Andy was surprised that people actually believed this. But he reflected that the real story wasn't all that easy to accept either.

They turned the corner of the ramparts. Below them Lachtenslachter was having an animated conversation with Doctor MacGool. "Everyone is concerned with building a better mousetrap. But we've got to think outside the box. The real trick is build a better mouse. Now with the new micro surgical techniques ..."

"I guess they've settled their differences," Cordy said.

"Yeah, MacGool is pretty happy. Waxroth offered him a lot of money to keep quiet about the unicorn brain. Except MacGool turned it down."

"He did?"

"He said that as the track vet it violated his professional ethics to accept money from gamblers. But he demanded the brain back for his collection after the Roan Ranger dies." Andy shook his head grimly. "I guess that won't be very long. Poor guy."

Cordy gave him a curious look. "Why do you say that?"

"Don't you think Waxroth is going to slaughter the Roan Ranger? I mean, he really hates that horse. We both know that."

"You're right. He *was* going to send it to the knackers," said Cordy. She smiled. "But greed got the better of him. It's just too valuable as a racehorse. I persuaded him that he might even earn some of his money back."

"What!" Andy stepped back and looked at her. She wasn't joking. "You went and talked to him!"

"I like the Roan Ranger. He's got a bad temper, and he's hard to control, but he never tried to throw me. He's basically a good horse. I didn't want to see him killed. And besides," she continued. "Waxroth is going to hire me to ride him."

"I don't believe this. You're going to ride for Waxroth?"

"He can't get anyone else. Sure, there might be other young jockeys out there who fit the bill, but if he starts asking around he's going to give away his secret. He has no choice. If he wants to maintain his tough guy image, he has to hire me. So, of course, I tripled my fee."

"But he broke your arm!"

"Yes, but what else can I do? I can't break his arm in revenge. I'd like to try, but he has bodyguards."

"Plus, you're a tad smaller than he is."

"Why yes, I suppose there's that, too. Good point. So taking his money is the only revenge I'll get. And the Roan Ranger has to race to live. The only reason that any owner, no matter who he is, keeps his horses alive is the hope that they'll win races. They're too expensive to keep otherwise."

It was an entirely reasonable, entirely logical answer. And like most reasonable, logical solutions, it wasn't very satisfying. Andy rolled it around in his head for a minute, and eventually shrugged. "It's your career, I guess." They crossed back to the ramparts at the front of the castle. Down below, Finishline and Goldie were moving their trunks into their cart. "Is MacGool going to let the Roan Ranger race?"

"Oh, sure. He said there was no doping or fraud involved, so he had no grounds to disqualify it."

"Hmm. I can think of another reason he wants it to race. His collection will get a unicorn brain that is also a famous racehorse brain. It will be extra unique."

Finishline and Goldie looked up and waved.

"Let's see if they want any help," said Andy.

But by the time they got downstairs Finishline already had the trunks loaded. Andy helped him harness up the cart horse. There were farewell hugs and handshakes all around. Finishline presented Andy with a pouch of coins.

"What's this?"

"This is your payment for riding the Roan Ranger, of course. Surely you did not think I was going to stiff you?"

"No, but ... I lost the race. I lost the horse. I botched the whole thing."

"Not for us, you didn't," Goldie told him. She took the money and put it in Andy's hand. "The jockey gets paid whether he wins or not. Even if he's thrown."

"I'm sorry, Andy." Cordy took the pouch of coins away from Andy and gave it back to Goldie. "Andy was entered as an amateur jockey. He doesn't get paid."

"That's fine with me," Andy told them. "Doctor Lachtenslachter covered my expenses. No problem."

"And this," Finishline said, producing another pouch of coins, "is your fee for training the horse."

"Thank you," said Cordy, accepting it without hesitation.

"Where are you going?" Andy asked Finishline.

"Ah." Finishline put his arm around Goldie's waist and drew her close to him. "For our first stop we are doing something very special. For my ever–loving girlfriend and I are engaged many years now, and this is something that I am promising her for a very long time."

Goldie opened her mouth in surprise. "Oh, Finishline!" She put her arms around him.

"You are most deserving of it, sweetheart." He kissed her once on each cheek. "I know what I am about to say is something you are waiting for me to say for a very long time, and I know that I am greatly remiss in not following through with this sooner. But now we are flush with cash money and it is a most beautiful day and furthermore you are looking particularly lovely at this time, and therefore I think we have no better option than to ride over to Farlong and do that thing that I know you are dreaming about."

"Oh Finishline! Do you really mean it?"

"Yes, sweetheart. We are going to the pawnshops to get back some of your jewelry."

Goldie's eyes were shining. "Finishline, you are so romantic."

Andy and Cordy watched their cart wend its way down the mountainside. "True love," Cordy sighed. "It's kind of—you know—icky."

"Why do I have the feeling they'll be broke again in six months?"

"Six months! Ha! I give them six weeks."

Lachtenslachter came up behind them, carrying a basket. He looked perplexed. "Andy, the grocery boy was just here. Do you know who ordered all these cherries?"

"Um, I think that might be Eddie." Andy took the basket from Lachtenslachter. "I'll bring this to him, Doctor Lachtenslachter"

"I had no idea he liked cherries that much."

"Um, they must be an acquired taste." Andy left Lachtenslachter and went to the rose garden. Cordy followed him. They found Eddie and Diana sitting on a stone bench in the middle of the garden.

"I was totally surprised," Diana was telling Eddie. "All this time I figured you for the sensitive musician type."

"Surprised about what? I *am* the sensitive musician type. Sensitivity is my middle name. And I mean that literally. I got a court order to have it legally changed to Sensitivity. Before that it was Arnold."

"But you're a fighter too." Diana was wearing a summer dress, a pink and white number of lightweight cotton that rippled in the wind, displaying enticing flashes of leg. She wrapped her delicate hands around one of Eddie's biceps. "I had no idea you were such a tough guy."

"You mean that thing with his arm? At the racetrack?" Eddie grinned. "I hate to admit it, Diana, but that's the only martial arts move I know. And I learned it from Andy." He kissed her on the nose, very gently. It had swollen up the day after Waxroth hit her. Now it looked almost normal, but it was still a little sensitive.

Cordy came up behind Andy and pressed against his back. "Get closer. I can't hear what they're saying."

"They're talking," Andy whispered back. "Don't you want to give them their privacy?"

"Of course I do! Just move a little closer so I can hear."

Andy looked at the couple sitting on the bench. Diana had her hand under Eddie's shirt once again, and was tracing lines across his skin. Cordy made a "tsk" sound. "Honestly, the way those two have been carrying on. Can you understand what he sees in her?"

"What?" said Andy. "You really don't know?"

"Yes, of course I do. I was just hoping you wouldn't."

Andy took her arm and led her out of the garden "Come on. Let us let them have their time together."

"What is she doing?" Cordy looked back over her shoulder.

"She's just caressing his scars. What bothers me," he said, trying to change the subject. "Is that we never found out just what Waxroth did to the race. What horse was his secret ringer? Was it Dental Carrie?"

Cordy had to think about it. "I suppose. He could have bribed all the other jockeys to slow their horses and to let her through. But Dental Carrie was always a strong finisher anyway. We'll have to accept that we're never going to find out."

"Okay, then. I think we've had a pretty good summer so far." Andy ticked off the items on his fingers. "Doctor Lachtenslachter's experiment was a success. We saved the life of a racehorse that otherwise would have gone to the glue factory. Doctor MacGool gets a more famous brain for his collection. Finishline and Goldie get their debts cleared. Waxroth has to pay a lot of money. The two thugs that messed with us both got their butts kicked. Eddie and Diana... um."

"Hooked up," Cordy suggested.

"Right. And you get a contract to race the fastest horse in Travaillia. So it's just a win, win, win, win, win and win situation all the way through. Is that right? Do I have enough wins?"

"Wait! What did you get out of all this?"

"That's the best part." Andy put his arms over his head and arched his back, feeling the muscles stretch. He gave Cordy a satisfied smile. "If the Roan Ranger hadn't thrown me, I probably would have spent the next ten years worried about my back, not riding or doing anything risky. Now I know I can do anything anyone else can do. So the race was a turning point for me."

"That's good."

"Plus, there was something else."

"What?"

"I got to kiss a beautiful girl."

"Oh really?" Cordy looked back over her shoulder, to where Eddie and Diana were still cuddling in the rose garden. "Only one?"

"Only one that counted."

"Oh really? And which one was that, may I ask?"

"Let me see." Andy turned to face her. He put his hands on her waist. She edged closer to him. "I think she has short hair."

"Mmm," said Cordy. Andy put his arm around her waist. She leaned her head against his shoulder. They both looked toward the stable yard, where Deedee was playing with Patches. "We'll have to get him back, you know."

"I know."

"I mean the Roan Ranger."

"I know."

"It's a good contract for me, Andy, but the Roan Ranger deserves a better owner than Werner Waxroth."

"I know. I'm thinking about it." Andy gave her a quick kiss. "Don't worry about it, Cordy. There's still plenty of summer left."

About the Author

The Lightning Horse is John Moore's his sixth novel—he has also had numerous short stories published in science fiction magazines and anthologies. You can find out more on his web page at www.sff.net/people/John.Moore.

About the Cover Artist

Brad W. Foster is an award-winning artist who has had work published in over a thousand books, magazines, comics, and indefinable small press publications—the man needs a hobby!

Brad has created nine covers for Yard Dog Press publications—*Illusions of Sanity, Wolf's Trap, Hammer Town, Dadgum Martians Invade the Lucky Nickel Saloon, Fairy BrewHaHa at the Lucky Nickel Saloon, Jaguar Moon, Bride of Tranquility, The Anthology from Hell,* and now *The Lightning Horse.*

Brad draws to live and finds it interesting that he also lives to draw. You can find out even more about Brad and his work at: http://www.jabberwockygraphix.com.

Yard Dog Press Titles As Of This Print Date

A Bubba In Time Saves None, Edited by Selina Rosen
A Glimpse of Splendor and Other Stories, Dave Creek
A Man, A Plan, (yet lacking) A Canal, Panama, Linda Donahue
Adventures of the Irish Ninja, Selina Rosen
The Alamo and Zombies, Jean Stuntz
All the Marbles, Dusty Rainbolt
Almost Human, Gary Moreau
Ancient Enemy, Lee Killouth
The Anthology From Hell: Humorous Tales From WAY Down Under, Edited by Julia S. Mandala
Assassins Inc., Phillip Drayer Duncan
Ard Magister, Laura J. Underwood
Bad Lands, Selina Rosen & Laura J. Underwood
Bad City, Selina Rosen & Laura J. Underwood
Black Rage, Selina Rosen
Blackrose Avenue, Mark Shepherd
The Boat Man, Selina Rosen
Bobby's Troll, John Lance
Bride of Tranquility, Tracy S. Morris
Bruce and Roxanne Save the World... Again!, Rie Sheridan
The Bubba Chronicles, Selina Rosen
Bubbas Of the Apocalypse, Edited by Selina Rosen
Chains of Redemption, Selina Rosen
Checking On Culture, Lee Killough
Chronicles of the Last War, Laura J. Underwood
Dadgum Martians Invade the Lucky Nickel Saloon, Ken Rand
Dark & Stormy Nights, Bradley H. Sinor
Deja Doo, Edited by Selina Rosen
Dracula's Lawyer, Julia S. Mandala
The Essence of Stone, Beverly A. Hale
Fairy BrewHaHa at the Lucky Nickel Saloon, Ken Rand
The Fantastikon: Tales of Wonder, Robin Wayne Bailey
Fire & Ice, Selina Rosen
Flush Fiction, Volume I: Stories To Be Read In One Sitting, Edited by Selina Rosen
The Four Bubbas of the Apocalypse: Flatulence, Halitosis, Incest, and... Ned, Edited by Selina Rosen
The Four Redheads: Apocalypse Now!, Linda L. Donahue, Rhonda Eudaly, Julia S. Mandala, & Dusty Rainbolt
The Four Redheads of the Apocalypse, Linda L. Donahue, Rhonda Eudaly, Julia S. Mandala, & Dusty Rainbolt
The Garden In Bloom, Jeffrey Turner
The Geometries of Love: Poetry by Robin Wayne Bailey

The Golems Of Laramie County, Ken Rand
The Green Women, Laura J. Underwood
The Guardians, Lynn Abbey
Hammer Town, Selina Rosen
The Happiness Box, Beverly A. Hale
The Host Series: The Host, Fright Eater, Gang Approval, Selina Rosen
Houston, We've Got Bubbas!, Edited by Selina Rosen
How I Spent the Apocolypse, Selina Rosen
I Didn't Quite Make It To Oz, Edited by Selina Rosen
I Should Have Stayed In Oz, Edited by Selina Rosen
Illusions of Sanity, James K. Burk
In the Shadows, Bradley H. Sinor
International House of Bubbas, Edited by Selina Rosen
It's the Great Bumpkin, Cletus Brown!, Katherine A. Turski
The Killswitch Review, Steven-Elliot Altman & Diane DeKelb-Rittenhouse
The Leopard's Daughter, Lee Killough
The Lightning Horse, John Moore
The Logic of Departure, Mark W. Tiedemann
The Long, Cold Walk To Mars, Jeffrey Turner
Marking the Signs and Other Tales Of Mischief, Laura J. Underwood
Material Things, Selina Rosen
Medieval Misfits: Renaissance Rejects, Tracy S. Morris
Mirror Images, Susan Satterfield
More Stories That Won't Make Your Parents Hurl, Edited by Selina Rosen
Music for Four Hands, Louis Antonelli & Edward Morris
My Life with Geeks and Freaks, Claudia Christian
The Necronomicrap: A Guide To Your Horoooscope, Tim Frayser
Playing With Secrets, Bradley H & Sue P. Sinor
Redheads In Love, Linda L. Donahue, Rhonda Eudaly, Julia S. Mandala, & Dusty Rainbolt
Reruns, Selina Rosen
Rock 'n' Roll Universe, Ken Rand
Shadows In Green, Richard Dansky
Some Distant Shore, Dave Creek
Stories That Won't Make Your Parents Hurl, Edited by Selina Rosen
Strange Twists Of Fate, James K. Burk
Tales From the Home for Wayward Spirits and Bar-B-Que Grill, Rie Sheridan

Tales from Keltora, Laura J. Underwood
Tales Of the Lucky Nickel Saloon, Second Ave., Laramie, Wyoming, U S of A, Ken Rand
Texistani: Indo-Pak Food From A Texas Kitchen, Beverly A. Hale
That's All Folks, J. F. Gonzalez
Through Wyoming Eyes, Ken Rand
Turn Left to Tomorrow, Robin Wayne Bailey
Wandering Lark, Laura J. Underwood
Wings of Morning, Katharine Eliska Kimbriel
Zombies In Oz and Other Undead Musings, Robin Wayne Bailey

Double Dog (A YDP Imprint):

#1:
Of Stars & Shadows,
Mark W. Tiedemann
This Instance Of Me,
Jeffrey Turner

#2:
Gods and Other Children,
Bill D. Allen
Tranquility,
Tracy Morris

#3:
Home Is the Hunter,
James K. Burk
Farstep Station,
Lazette Gifford

#4:
Sabre Dance,
Melanie Fletcher
The Lunari Mask,
Laura J. Underwood

#5:
House of Doors,
Julia Mandala
Jaguar Moon,
Linda A. Donahue

Just Cause (A YDP Imprint):

Death Under the Crescent Moon
Dusty Rainbolt

The Ghost Writer
Selina Rosen

It's Not Rocket Science: Spirituality for the Working-Class Soul
Selina Rosen

Not My Life
Selina Rosen

The Pit
Selina Rosen

Plots and Protagonists: A Reference Guide for Writers
Mel. White

Vanishing Fame
Selina Rosen

Non-YDP titles we distribute:

Chains of Freedom
Chains of Destruction
Jabone's Sword
Queen of Denial
Recycled
Strange Robby
Sword Masters
Selina Rosen

Three Ways to Order:

1. Write us a letter telling us what you want, then send it along with your check or money order (made payable to Yard Dog Press) to: Yard Dog Press, 710 W. Redbud Lane, Alma, AR 72921-7247

2. Use selinarosen@cox.net or lynnstran@cox.net to contact us and place your order. Then send your check or money order to the address above. *This has the advantage of allowing you to check on the availability of short-stock items such as T-shirts and back-issues of Yard Dog Comics.*

3. Contact us as in #1 or #2 above and pay with a credit card or by debit from your checking account. Either give us the credit card information in your letter/Email/phone call, or go to our website and use our shopping carts. If you send us your information, please include your name as it appears on the card, your credit card number, the expiration date, and the 3 or 4-digit security code after your signature on the back (CVV). Please remember that we will include media rate (minimum $3.00) S/H for mailing in the lower 48 states.

Watch our website at
www.yarddogpress.com
for news of upcoming projects
and new titles!!

A Note to Our Readers

We at Yard Dog Press understand that many people buy used books because they simply can't afford new ones. That said, and understanding that not everyone is made of money, we'd like you to know something that you may not have realized. Writers only make money on new books that sell. At the big houses a writer's entire future can hinge on the number of books they sell. While this isn't the case at Yard Dog Press, the honest truth is that when you sell or trade your book or let many people read it, the writer and the publishing house aren't making any money.

As much as we'd all like to believe that we can exist on love and sweet potato pie, the truth is we all need money to buy the things essential to our daily lives. Writers and publishers are no different.

We realize that these "freebies" and cheap books often turn people on to new writers and books that they wouldn't otherwise read. However we hope that you will reconsider selling your copy, and that if you trade it or let your friends borrow it, you also pass on the information that if they really like the author's work they should consider buying one of their books at full price sometime so that the writer can afford to continue to write work that entertains you.

We appreciate all our readers and *depend* upon their support.

Thanks,
The Editorial Staff
Yard Dog Press

PS – Please note that "used" books without covers have, in most cases, been stolen. Neither the author nor the publisher has made any money on these books because they were supposed to be pulped for lack of sales.

Please do not purchase books without covers.

Printed in Great Britain
by Amazon.co.uk, Ltd.,
Marston Gate.